D1593908

REPUBLICS OF REALITY

BOOKS BY CHARLES BERNSTEIN

Parsing (Asylum's Press, 1976)
Shade (Sun & Moon Press, 1978)
Poetic Justice (Pod Books, 1979)
Senses of Responsibility (Tuumba Press, 1979)
Legend [with Bruce Andrews, Ray DiPalma, Steve McCaffery, and Ron Silliman] (L=A=N=G=U=A=G=E/Segue, 1980)
Controlling Interests (Roof Books, 1980)
Disfrutes (Potes and Poets Press, 1981)
The Occurrence of Tune [with Susan Bee] (Segue, 1981)
Stigma (Station Hill Press, 1981)
Islets/Irritations (Jordan Davies, 1983; reprinted by Roof Books, 1992)
Resistance (Awede Press, 1983)
Content's Dream: Essays 1975–1984 (Sun & Moon Press, 1985)
Veil (Xexoxial Editions, 1987)
The Sophist (Sun & Moon Press, 1987)
The Nude Formalism [with Susan Bee] (Sun & Moon Press, 1989)
The Absent Father in Dumbo (Zasterle, 1990)
Rough Trades (Sun & Moon Press, 1991)
A Poetics (Harvard University Press, 1992)
Dark City (Sun & Moon Press, 1994)
The Subject (Meow, 1995)
Little Orphan Anagram [with Susan Bee] (Granary Books, 1997)
Log Rhythms [with Susan Bee] (Granary Books, 1998)
Reading Red [with Richard Tuttle] (Köln: Walther Konig, 1998)
My Way: Speeches and Poems (The University of Chicago Press, 1999)
Republics of Reality: 1975–1995 (Sun & Moon Press, 2000)

Editor

99 Poets/1999: An International Poetics Symposium
(a special issue of *boundary 2*, 1999)
Close Listening: Poetry and the Performed Word (Oxford University Press, 1998)
The Politics of Poetic Form: Poetry and Public Policy (Roof Books, 1990)
L=A=N-G=U=A=G=E [with Bruce Andrews] (1978–1981)

CHARLES BERNSTEIN

Republics of Reality

1975–1995

LOS ANGELES
SUN & MOON PRESS
2000

Sun & Moon Press
A Program of The Contemporary Arts Educational Project, Inc.
a nonprofit corporation
6026 Wilshire Boulevard, Los Angeles, California 90036
www.sunmoon.com

This edition first published in 2000 by Sun & Moon Press
10 9 8 7 6 5 4 3 2 1
FIRST EDITION

©1976, 1978, 1979, 1981, 1983, 1990, 2000 by Charles Bernstein
Biographical material ©2000 by Sun & Moon Press
All rights reserved

For Susan Bee

Republics of Reality: 1975–1995 brings together works written between
1975 and 1995. The book reprints eight previously published books; the author
would like to thank the publishers. The ninth section, *Residual Rubbernecking,*
appears here for the first time in book form; the poems in that series
originally appeared in *"90," Aerial, Archive for New Poetry Newsletter* (UCSD),
*Avec, The Baffler, Big Allis, boundary 2, Colorado North Review,
Columbia Poetry Review, Contemporanea, Critical Quarterly, Harvard Magazine,
Long News, Michigan Quarterly Review, Mudfish, No Roses Review,
Object Permanence, Poetry Project Newsletter, Postmodern Culture, Private, River Styx,
Sam Change Tense: Poems for Samuel Beckett, A Salt Reader, Talisman,
Tongue to Boot, Turbulence, University Libraries Christmas Broadside* (SUNY-Buffalo),
Uprising, The World, River City, and in *Four Poems* (Chax Press, 1988) and
Little Orphan Anagram (Granary Books, 1997).

Cover: Susan Bee, *To the Lighthouse II,* 1981
Design: Katie Messborn
Typography: Guy Bennett

LIBRARY OF CONGRESS CATALOGING IN PUBLICATION DATA
Bernstein, Charles [1950]
Republics of Reality: 1975–1995
p. cm _ (Sun & Moon Classics: 120)
ISBN: 1-55713-304-2
I. Title. II. Series.
811'.54_dc20

Printed in the United States of America on acid-free paper.

Without limiting the rights under copyright reserved here,
no part of this publication may be reproduced, stored in or introduced into
a retrieval system, or transmitted, in any form or by any means
(electronic, mechanical, photocopying, recording or otherwise),
without the prior written permission of both the copyright owner
and the above publisher of the book.

Contents

Parsing

1
9
7
6

I • SENTENCES

It's an automatic thing. It doesn't require any thought. It's a parade in and out.

It has its ups and downs.

It doesn't affect me one way or another.

○ ● ○

It sort of comes to you. I never look at it. The touch. My hands fit. It's the feel. I just look at them.

○ ● ○

It'll sound terrible. It's true. It's nothing really. I like to fuss. I sit and relax and read, take a bath, have my ice cream. I fill the day.

You look around. You hear things. Sometimes you daydream you're really somebody special. It's the sort of thing you do.

I could never converse with anyone about it.

It would drive me nuts. It would drive me wild. I

know I'm needed. I think a lot. I have very simple pleasures. I'm not a deep reader. I can't understand a lot of things. I'm looking forward to it.

o ● o

I always have a hard time saying it. It feels too personal. It seems inconsequential. It keeps me from knowing what to do.

It really get to me.
It do something to me.

They want you to clean.
They don't have no feeling.
They want to know "what should I call you?"
They stand and look at you like you crazy.

You can't take pride anymore.

You remember when a guy could point to a house he built.

You never see the end result of it.

You fend it off as much as you can.

You think of a perpetual vacation.

You just get used to it.

o ● o

I become very upset.

            I enjoy one thing more than another.

        I think I'm much happier.

         I have dinner.

             I like the background music.

          I don't become bored with it.

I find it very discouraging.

I get no word from her.

I don't like all this waiting.

I feel she's not very considerate of me.

I feel left out.

I know it doesn't necessarily mean anything.

I wish all this could work out better.

I want by now to get some clear idea of where we are in respect to each other.

It seems so indeterminate.

It seems so uncertain.

You think of bringing back together all the people you ever knew.

You think of how it feels to be together again.

You try somehow to escape the fact of its absence, of its flight, of its no longer being there.

You write letters.

You call people up.

You hurriedly meet with people.

You hope to find it.

You hope it will return.

You make fun of yourself.

You say it isn't so serious.

You try to be ironic.

○ ● ○

You try to keep from going crazy with boredom.

You become accustomed as time goes by.

You read magazines.

You sleep.

You do anything to keep from going nuts.

You're very much occupied.

You're fighting to maintain your speed.

You have to be superalert all the time.

You have to anticipate situations a block ahead of you.

You have to get all psyched up.

You always give that smile.

You say to yourself one day my time will come.

You try to show a cockiness like you could care less.

You get in deeper and deeper.

I feel too dependent.

I feel no sense of myself.

I continually need reassurance.

I feel she won't really express her feelings.

I feel shut out.

I can project everything and be reassured of nothing.

I am constantly feeling left.

I see in her silence and distance the same fear and pain I have.

I see how much she means to them.

I expect to be refused.

I feel an intruder.

I see her pulling back.

I just can't keep being understanding.

I'll be disappointed, crushed.

I don't want to go through it again.

I don't exactly know how to act.

I came up the hard way. We was treated pretty rough. We come up at the hind and get what we can to live on. We was just children.

I just sit here and think about it. I just wonder all about it. I wonder what people mean. I just thinks about all that. That's all I can tell you. My mind goes but my mind comes to me. I'm just here.

There was this man. All I wanted to do was see the man.
He had these little trees. He was telling us to come into
the boat. I asked Mama could I go down there.

He carried us down there and showed us things down
there.

o ● o

He named me Charley.

o ● o

He was dying and he called for me. He said, "Bring me
the holy bible with all y'alls names in it." And he was
dying and he said to me, "Don't break your oath: don't
change your name don't change your name." And I
stooped over him and put his arm around my neck. And
when he quit saying that he was dead. And I shook him.

I'm separated.

I would put myself in suspended animation.

I was never home.

you say to yourself is it me is it my fault is it something i'm mistaking or getting wrong or failing to see

it comes all about as bleakness, you never feel as rich but in the emptiness, seeing a few things, one or two, and being almost overwhelmed.

people come in, you talk to them, you wonder if they really are seeing the same things, if they are willing

you design patterns to get it all down, you stay up all night trying to figure out the puzzles you've created for yourself, you can't understand why so few care, you forget about what you were thinking and can't remember

you say to yourself let it go but you can't figure out what to let go

I didn't sleep those nights.

I wanted to go and do things.

I don't feel that lonely.

I don't bother the nurses.

I kind of have to grit my teeth.

I never have anyone to share it with.

I have gone into intense pain.

I have talked that over.

I don't really know.

I liked books and things.

I would have been a good mother.

I crank the bed down.

I'm not so young.

I had to evaluate my faith.

I had to become what everyone wanted me to be.

I had the fever and the chills.

I developed nodes again.

I've noticed it.

I would feel guilty.

I was the only one in the family.

I felt like a leper.

I have done everything I possibly could.

I don't know why.

I thought this was kind of typical.

I need people.

I look at the young people.

I'm not going to change my language.

I said nothing to anyone.

I really have a problem understanding all of these things.

I was in a room.

I have walked.

I didn't really feel too well.

I'm not afraid.

I ask for a pain pill.

I felt this out.

I'm glad for what I've got.

I do it in pain.

I think that is all good for me.

I had to remind them.

I think they resented it very much.

I refused.

I get up.

I feel a part of life.

I can go to my room.

I can bear it.

I've watched.

I had so much pain I couldn't breathe.

I dread loneliness.

I mean it was a compulsion.

I could have really used a backrub.

I have gotten panicky.

I felt that no one was around.

I put on the light and waited.

I'm glad I have done everything I possibly could.

I have a sense of accomplishment.

I am aware of these things.

I need these things.

I wanted to give myself to God.

I see the difference now.

I was groping to understand.

I looked at him.

I was so different.

I went on thinking.

I joined different clubs.

I wondered if it would get me somewhere where I would stand out.

I was not behaving myself.

I would allow people to come in my room.

I could be there.

I would find it a barrier.

I found it hard all my life.

I didn't understand.

I don't begrudge other people.

I did it freely.

I really mean it.

I hate it so much.

I do not often find a person who can talk to me beyond ordinary conversation.

I must convey to others that I don't need them.

I don't think this should be necessary.

I think they should be aware.

I'm not trying to hide anything.

I've been very ill.

I would stand in front of the desk.

I had a rash all over my body.

I was always trying my hardest.

I felt it.

I didn't think I had more than a year to live.

I went and looked it up.

I didn't have to convince anybody.

I found it so hard.

I was starting to teach.

I had somebody else's religion.

I was attracted to these things.

I had to almost hide all my sores.

I am in tears.

I had never really met people like this.

I know I have to do something.

I can forget my problems.

I could ask.

I can talk as simply to a child as anyone else can.

I take the blanket out.

I didn't necessarily make them angry.

I do receive a lot.

I couldn't discuss it anymore with people.

I had what I said I had.

I didn't feel accepted.

I needed to be treated.

I've been up.

I have to do it slowly.

I do better on my own.

I can't beg them for it.

I don't even like the word.

I need it.

I have pain.

I go back to work.

I appreciate their understanding.

I'm going to sweat.

I

I am ashamed.

I hide.

I felt my life with both my hands.

I had not minded walls.

I felt a cleaving in my mind.

I tie my hat.

I crease my shawl.

I cross till I am weary.

I felt as if the grass were pleased.

I cannot buy it.

I know some lonely houses off the road.

I watched the moon and the house.

I learned at last what home could be.

I lived on dread.

I stood up.

I measure every grief.

I heard as I had no ear.

I held a jewel in my fingers.

I cannot tell you but you feel it.

2

It always felt to me wrong.

It bloomed and dropt.

It ceased to hurt me.

It knew no lapse or diminution.

It knew no medicine.

It rises.

It sifts.

It struck me every day.

It tossed and tossed.

It was not death.

It's like the light.

II • PARSING

the reach, the middle, endless, drift, sway, hold, belie
unfold and furl, it makes, smack, abated,

        against at top

what, and frap
      jimmie, ice blue,

       the. It sat

          sometimes, among

     who on

           could, semblance

           of narrow

    land, larger, riddling

      axe, they

      _____

so its i don't want to work there you plunge in you do
anything you can to keep from going nuts you write it
down you go to the store with it it persists as thickness as
shape as figments and fragments of refusal you stare at it &
by the time you notice you have lost your comprehension
    wanting to see event k but despairing of its possibilities
                it doesn't work
        too many refusals,
                    poetic
                    & flat surfaceless ridgeless
                            degree zero is marked
                    ashen
            is so many times reaching, pouring
                            in tuppats
            a man, son, millionaire
    "a capital assets tax"
                —they don't play that way
                    & i sat & i listened & i behaved myself
                being in the presence of
                            telling me how to live to go on
        it, solemn
            its vacancy
                too many now and i cldn't choose because
always there was unclarity how do i approach this how do i
go on am i seeing things okay the blind reb who wants love
attention wants to be seen battered unbroken

————————

an inability, of warmth, that blasts, the old j d thats,
popping, pouring, get going, getting started, trying to lose
sense, lose consciousness, myrrh, warmth, an occlusion,
blotting, test pattern,
                    amazing can only remember what has been
previously written so a repeating and continual reference,
unable to make progress, to move ahead, wanting each
thing to be a new thing, to be perfect, to be interesting,
stellar, a gem, full of crystals and obsessiveness
  so that they give you a free dinner, an echo, a chant,
        but insecure, giving up on the prior and trying the
inherent, what gives or comes, set on puerility, boredom,
non-interest, a desperation that communication will fail
for lack of direction,   he plays the piano, the harp,
harmonium, flute, lute, and loses track, key, treble
        much too hard, to know, to want to give it over, to
find place,   is a delusion
      simply cant keep up with itself
                          "& weep"
    an excitement of adulthood
                    "look how many keys i have so that shows
                    i'm important, i have entry
                              & they care"

  they blast, keep it,
              its not even them liking me but my being able to
care about them, to feel it, and then its not enough,
because by then all the force bottled up explodes and fills
up the other, becomes fixated, transfixed

   so you get so and its all blithering and its all
just endless figments, fragments, the
    to get it, it

———

you cant insure it in the same way that you cant necessarily
go to sleep at will, at the drop of a hat
          to begin a topic, misplacing, miscatching, nouns,
that is calling a peach a pear with absolute conviction, like
mistyping an l instead of an e, why so peculiar, that e, l,

     placing the jug on the table

               always the loudness of on, that quiet seems less a
zen, exchange, bracelet

                    ovular containment

                    till it comes,   somehow in the taping,
performance, i felt continuously called upon, demanded of,
that it was necessary to act without particularly the good
fortune to know how to act

                         he placed the jug on the table

          & still this sense of sense leaves residue
of personal taste, odor, that blocks from its granite
like figment, blankness, frozen shape

was invited, called to attend, was involved
in that shrine, feign, meeting ground
& F___ & W___ & M___,
all necessary to this,
in this
light, air, substance

———

to fill up this

was a man sitting there
without program, rule

abiding

was a grouper hence graphic

makes no cohesion

world, waste,

too its too

i placed the jug on the table

placing the jug on the table

i was placing the jug on the table

hence graphic, grouper

a graphic

a piston

a placement

of the jug on the

sitting, without program, abiding

a gunge hence grouper

placing, hence

piston, gunge

the jug coming upon the table,

surfacing with it

————————

was pealing an apricot
was pealing an american
was pealing a jug, sitting,
        setting, the apricot
was pealing a fig
was pealing,
     very sorrowful, she said,
         in itself
        was standing
        was luminous
        was a kirelian photoillumination
        was beautiful

  "it's more than that, than anything," _____ explained joyfully
            & sat down
              head bare,

        & more than that it
           does not change
               though its patterns
           vary, recur
             in illuminations
                 or occlusions, amid a
               field, grid
                 the mind is
                           as
            jug, fig, luminous

■

                              was aztec
                              was sock
                              was misplaced

    hence polyhedron, figment,
                      lemon, limit
              vagrancy

              was a sign
              was painted
              was glassy

                          & slipped in it

                    _____

so you sit down, they say, & wait for it

      stripping the bass on the beach,
            peeling the skin off,
                cooking it & eating it,

        was a tall one, they say
        was fat, they say
        was in a blue robe or hunting vestment

& then walk around, looking
        & leave the room

        they say it's

     & the bones unnerve yr tongue
        you spit them out

           sitting down, you run out of content

     yr tongue in its mouth
     cheeks inert

           going into the space outside
             yr body spilling out of doors

     as though,

———

the dishes, piling
the work refused

piles, clump, clot

                contextual disruption
                contextual disruption
                contextual disruption

        having robbed my self

                    of illusion, chimera

                    wild insistence on
            being there,

                    here, as
            progression to opal

                        i cld not paint a picture

    … i cld not live with you

                    knowing then the

            circumference of an

                    opal is

bounded by disruption

"i did not drag my father beyond this tree"

———

was waiting

was jumping around

was giving it up

      across

          speed, struck,

      & then

was tasting

was a jack in the box

saw a stuffed pig

      dry,

        "to like from being"

   is an attraction

      to rudeness, fixation

         an intimacy or sense of outside

■

an edge

coming to meet

only the talking no more than the waiting for speech,
an emptiness i bring to it, or both together, in the
interpretation, always seeing as, & as absence

———————

but what

    at least a person's gotta work,

        eat, wear clothing

      at least a person wants to feel a part

    to sometimes have a place to sit

      to sit down

      to place oneself in a chair

sitting,

trying to stand up,

peeling an apple,

    at least one has a need for

        (a sense of)

      space

  & is veiled

"deep
 the abyss
 calls to deep"

               as if in peeling
               the fruit was compromised

    so among

        & seeing within

      the method of sight

                    is ingrained

               fixed as shrine

                     grid, map

            in which we

                               as a pear is succulent

                               or a ball divine

                  is pen

                  is key

■

is this, in particular

& so lets say

_____

"I remember
 the pearls that were his eyes"
        how they shone

                with the he, she & it of it

        as if,

                seeing as,

        they stood alone.

    I remember how her hair, tangled,

                so that she always was wanting to refuse

        & waiting, next to

                it occurred to me

                it made me unable to concentrate

                it made me want to forget about myself

    so that thinking as much as drinking in a stream
demanded a full measure of

                trout, they said,

■

"but i know you"

turning a bed down

or a deaf ear

"but won't you at least…"

ear drum, steel ear, ear ring

turning to

apple, peach,

fish wine,

_____

"What is the reason
  that as soon as someone
  expresses a need for
  another she draws away?"

          Gravity, that pulls down
                or away as fog.

     I can't feel what you're saying.

        I become frightened.

     My mind wanders.

          I think you don't care.

       I want you to listen to me,
            care about me.

               I want to hold on to your
weight, substance, the gleam i keep seeing

     & you say ———,

      but don't care about it,

        not caring if i'm convinced,
            if i get to know you

It is as if

    i want you

to get up close

        & look in.

————

the snow,

    flakes,

this parsing of the world

    to make worlds & worlds

like atmosphere

    a substance, of gravity

        that pulls apart

    or back on

i slept then, i bathed on wednesdays also

        the feta cheese

        the mozzarella marzipan

        the seedless eye brow pencils

    was waiting for the bust &

    was on a telephone,

        gyroscope, sleeping binge

■

was hiding in a rock,

crystal, postcard

was a blue flame,

a grammar booklet, an azure

azalia

————————

'The weight of a gaze
  conveys an intention,'

          substance, particular of consciousness,

                    located as the gravity of a space,

              thus composed

                        as seeing clumped with memory.

                    ∘ ● ∘

        An outside much colder

                    static, globous,

                    ∘ ● ∘

"They would demand to tell you how to look,"

                    shave, wear clothing,

            as if

          imperceptible,
            fixed as mode,

                    you could eat an orange

                                        ■

or peel a pear

without some longing for it

as an atmosphere is fixed,

charged with a static that binds,

as the head is pressed.

———————

Space and Poetry

space, and poetry

dying and transforming words, before

arbitrary, period locked

with meaning" and which

preposterousness. Still

the "energy" of a given

to be. After

changes. These changes

dislocated from any

sequence. If you are used

of obvious dialogue, the sermonizing

"type." But

events, and probability

consolatory asymptote

translucent pink ones

art, but an art

put upon it by

elements and operations. It is even easier

relating to truth (the object

which meaning is inferred, as in

openness. That they should appear

the mark of

recognizability. Sometimes only the attachment

across the board

between representations on

arrangement, of balance or equivocal balance

king." This hostility

or else a kind

■

concluded. By which

    centered around

  you'd say "that's

    up an image, not upon

■

Roseland

you need some way of

some set of

you live in a place

it isn't much

you move out

you have to

you live at the edge

your memory has let you down

a kind of chaos

when you go

if you face it

this axis this

the human order

more or less

you have a map

you put yourself in position

and try to

this is the

a human construction

you try out the space

try to

you drive on them

go straight

one might imagine

only grasping

a pity

a pile of rocks

more or less

and place the

wander for

not proceed

is still a little

an edge

unless the habit

land of

boomerang say

carvings

all of the circles

so that what we have is a network

and thats all

a sequence of camping sights

is arbitrarily adapted

■

which was shape

very much a matter of

there will be a woman

of anxiety which is to

the career

some premonition

the appearance of white

the fixing

when the time comes

edicts and statutes

in some unexplained

has the nostalgia

and thats

as talking

of some other blind man

exists in space

an overall kind of thing

cant flip

or more information of any kind

the passage is nothing

one thing in particular

a technique of erasing

and people could start

its not too

that is real

and how it

or you hope

you get ready

you work on it

a literal culture

■

a piece of sand

in such a

an elaborate way

an art of naming

a kind of

that is danced

as among

a residue

from the milk

notion of a

goes in

of entrance

if you use stone

as required

in such a system

you use language

or some set of

if you face it

Shade

I
9
7
8

Poem

here. Forget.

There are simply tones

cloudy, breezy

birds & so on.

Sit down with it.

It's time now.

There is no more natural sight.

Anyway transform everything

silence, trees

commitment, hope

this thing inside you

flow, this movement of eyes

set of words

all turns, all grains.

At night, shift

comets, "twirling planets,

suns, bits of illuminated pumice"

pointing out, in harsh tones

cancers & careers.

"Newer Limoges please."

Pick some value

mood, idea, type or smell of paper

iridescent, lackluster

&, "borne in peach vessels,"

just think

"flutter & cling"

with even heavier sweep

unassuaged

which are the things

of a form, etc

that inhere.

Fair adjustment

becomes space between

crusts of people

strange, rending:

a sound of some importance

diffuses

"as dark red circles"

digress, reverberate

connect, unhook.

Your clothes, for example

face, style

radiate mediocrity

coyly, slipping

& in how many minutes

body & consciousness

deflect, "flame on flare"

missed purpose.

Your eyes

glaze

thought stumbles, blinded

speck upon speck

ruffling edges.

"But do not be delighted yet."

The distance positively entrances.

Take out pad & pen

crystal cups, velvet ashtray

with the gentility of easy movement

evasive, unaccountable

& puffing signs

detach, unhinge

beyond weeds, chill

with enthusiastic smile

& new shoes

"by a crude rotation"

hang

a bulk of person

"ascending," "embodied."

Ballet Russe

Every person has feeling.

It is all the same.

I will travel.

I love nature.

I love motion & dancing.

I did not understand God.

I have made mistakes.

Bad deeds are terrible.

I suffered.

My wife is frightened.

The stock exchange is death.

I am against all drugs.

My scalp is strong & hard.

I like it when it is necessary.

It is a lovely drive.

A branch is not a root.

Handwriting is a lovely thing.

I like tsars & aristocrats.

An aeroplane is useful.

One should permanently help the poor.

My wife wants me to go to Zurich.

Politics are death.

All young men do silly things.

The Spaniards are terrible people because they murder bulls.

My wife suffered a great deal because of her mother.

I will tell the whole truth.

I love Russia.

I am nasty.

I am terrified of being locked up & losing my work.

Mental agony *is* a terrible thing.

I pretend to be a very nervous man.

of course

my writing

writing

even talking like this

always seems to me perfectly at peace

so that

I was thinking

I don't know

this could be my own you know

this could be sort of the

the source of my crazy hood/ness

that the things that are really valuable don't
so much happen as you experience them

in the actual present

a lot of what I experience

is a sense of space

& vacant space at that

sort of like a stanley kubrick film

sort of a lot of objects floating separately

which I don't particularly feel do anything for me

give me anything

make me feel good

& when I do feel almost best

is when I don't care

whether they make me feel good

whether they have any relation to me

that's a very pleasant

that's a real feeling of value

in the present moment

to just sit & do nothing

& that's what writing is for me a lot

or just sitting

sometimes when I

I sit in my office

with my eyes closed

on my chair

& let my mind wander

there's a certain sense of not caring

& letting it just go by

that I like

& then there is actual relationships

you know

sometimes

touching

whether it's listening to a piece of music

or talking to somebody a lot

being with certain people sometimes

but a lot of it has to do with memory

& remembering

that it was

it was something

that somehow the value seems to lie

historically

I look back

& I see things that really do seem

worthwhile

& worth it

& I see how things I am doing now

become things of worth

for instance

the way I behave

if I try to behave

well

decently

or justly

or whatever it is

that we take to be what we judge ourselves by

when we have a conversation

& we say

that's fucked & that's not

whatever we go by in that sense

I mean

making that happen

building that

it does seem

you know

worth

a value

funny refreshing

nice

wonderful

or a movie sometimes

moments

hours

days

months

& then

you know

even years

& lifetimes

sure

but

something

in

the

actual

experiencing

of

it

that does seem

vacant

in the way a lot

is vacant

but

also

the way

yeah

okay

new mexico

is

vacant

St. McC.

graphemic

hinges

discourse

re-ordering

SIGNS

of

few little

whch

speed &

wh.

inter-sentential

connexions

there's

splendid

"here too"

in

not forced

stuff

the rest of

· *piecemeal*

spins off

"ethical"

intrude

wiTh tHaT kiNd oF

schizophallic

categories

enfolding

a proper place

fix(ist) ⸺ *physicist*

opting for a

* * * * *

so find

isn't

TURN

face to a

inevitable

picturesque

baulk

DESIRE

tokened by

topology": the

se e

"OR"

verfrumsdungseffect

autonomous explosions

taste as

blocks, circling

like (star), fl…m…n…g…

aire, leap—

as if we had

not gleaned

in a "possible"

vectorate

these: the

issued

■

, canopy

as scratch (rune

potential a

s...n...r...ty

the pull

"buckle me"

with a ...pAt

    "i leap up"

sights

"iDeaLLy"

being (?)

"happens"

nOt sParTaN

: polish(s) (ed)

ll

TO FACE

ou///eg///t///

am (visit, subdue, impulse)

b...l...r...ty

For —————

> "as a tree is connected in its own
> roots so a person is connected in
> his/her own self"

touch. Obviously

what else, meaning

in comparison, I guess

complicating things at

distance. Your life seems

to let more than

things, like lovers

with it, though writing

caring enough & the

others of, wondering

created like: I have

part of. Gradually

burden you. What's

place? I fade like

but in a small way

[handwritten annotations: "language of sentiment fractured" and "saying some of things"]

scare me. Otherwise

images, finite, emptiness

of living in

caring about; are

now, felt, marks

to need you

distantly covers it

exactly; confirm that

as rejection (or am

saying (an now

friends; of each

being struck

& all

sounds; "flippance"; seams

amaze me

else. So it

pass deliberately

even

greed": that does

ease for which

internalness & possession

style, the art

remembrance of

posing, pretence

grip nor even

objects (chairs, faces, mountains

look at

optically

incredible, bitter

presence

of this

wasting away in

felt emotions. That's what

I think (must seem

& it. To time

that—back in

just kissing

but still—to you—become what

it now, I do

as rejection, that

with you

but put on

(whatever

"crush" is

that I like (you

always afraid that

now, exactly, I

confirm

in the new

visage of the place

is, it's more

by lacking

depersonalize it

else, to be alive

"in love" with

sleep, fast, &

hear your

role.) Anyway

relationships—so so—we

you, distantly, when

wonder at that gap

in time. Between

am, since

& especially acknowledge

much, but, this

envy

"as I'd be"

lashing at lack

need you (I

another person, everyone, is

"focused"

more & more, cling

—writing, moves, you

but obviously what's

as with new kinds of

which are living with

relations & ~~rejections~~

this—but this

in a different way

looks at

its worth

& if that's

over & above

again, here, I

perhaps tell you

I want to be trustworthy

&c

at, which is

of how things really

(not in my fashion

occur

& are occasionally

as well as usual

details in touch

make me

feel your sense of

things

whirling in response

isolate

listless, finally

in a characteristic way

its colors

transformed into vacancy

floating, airy

like a long time

unintimidated, unconditioned

you, those

for my part

persons (view of

grading importances

up, lately

as you

sad: completely

feel like

parts

at it always

life; got

of truncated

alternatives

still holds

as it says

months:

~~governs~~

things, necessarily

you, your

bring it on

mean its

complication

at

tangles

as truth

used

or easily

■

thought

of, yet

other persons

spoke, real, reason

a line. Left after

mystification & confusion

shifting responsibilities

"fluctuating" as you say

to) get

this kind of

continual missing

self-doubt, infatuation

stripped, down

& afraid, for instance

(gasps, what's

to say

"I should say"

& you, you

I feel (whether or not

is lost

up against

these lines

jags

for someone, to hear from

shapes me

'so that I will exist'

strange, the power

not in my fear

draws their meaning

all this. I

& that's

motion, the sight of birds

an externalization, all moving

as I have

not cloud, haze, or sadness

you, I

& speed with

in a way this whole

restores my balance

becomes reason

I was thinking

of rooms, inhabiting

& my friends

around

I always

the continual problem

of having done 'this'

seems to just

be, yet

telling you

wakes me.

***

& the tea cup

aerates

to the clicking radiator

"all pseudo-breaths"

smile, in perfect

nervous energy

of the recognition, obelisks

that blankly

fill our

pockets)

stencils of misprision

sharpen, convexly

& promised

sticks

as if

it, in that

way (person

saw that

there, I

kept (& yet

seemed, it became

so

persons to

(enough

fixed, immobile

am here

at an

know (especially

with. Somehow

above that

come. In this

which pulls

& say whatever, without

as now

for me, it makes

pale

"what has

in me

sunny, clear

loose & even

rusty

chatting, "please

to put on a

(as you say

good appearance

lonely & scared

but see under

(since

this, then

best as can

which is, so

"words, ashes"

meetings, beings

time—(all

in this, only

saying it, that

emptiness, dragged

the distance

sounded sad

an aberration

vanished

by looming

powerless. (At

front (i.e. your

as if I

out (an

weight, which

it then becomes

you?) you certainly

as much because

note, saw

& me off

there—but

talked of

now (just

fuzzy

days, &

remembering

feeling that placelessness

all around

personalities, friends, a place to live

I think we

anyway

measure of

other. You

mean—that is

want

(at least

some physical (ie present

aspect to it

visits, sometimes

see, touch, taste

is, with

eyes) desires

what they must feel

& not let

intensely, deeply

"too chill to spell"

be held

primarily

a kind of strength

frightens

one for each moment

conviction (don't

luminance, brilliance

—you can't deny it—

come

before I go crazy

of objects

where, here, in this

suddenly stands erect

with wanting

is the 'there'

rejection, love

it

by its nature

asserts

it sees

as fork a fork

& a bully

completely)—in other words:

a strange moment

& try to get inside that

(you can't completely

to take seriously

(sensationally, ironically

& pick up dish & chair

& through all of it

miss you

only that

but not quite

(I know sometime

you will explain, it's

to break

through this

& show how

it's happening

in each phrase

that I

can't hold you

look, in your

eyes, even

& my fantasy always is

but

if I could

would have no words

& yet sometimes

it seems

(I'm not saying

for me either

& beside that

coming, dealing

clinging, wondering

I just wish

sometimes

that we all

don't have to be

so caught up

yet, what, cut

out all this

confusion, complication

& really, what

is it

projection scares me

(simplicity

undisrupted, as if

need, that thing

"like they will

hurt so much

turn, & recalling

to satisfy

draw in, so

inside

belonging, & not

wanting

(I look everyday

as if the actuality

mythological, conceptual

taken just as that

cuts, edged

to get

at it

as much & more

this misses—

as whiff of air

shocks the senses, remembering

what it was

submerged

as that

enclosed, anxious

contemplation of

what, with

It's up up

    I skate across, feel skittish

      "there are limits to what I can put up with"

keep it here

     study, assuage,

        hold, slips

          a slippage

   automatic, recurrent

             grows typical, unworldly:

"voice, accent, manner, face, mind"

        look, sound, purpose.

 We insist formally on several elements.

     Truth, false starts, fresh starts

         "slow speed & heavy reason"

       to my lot,

         fell/

#23

seems, finally

it's there

& yet you're

exactly where

the peering

tangible

seems

after all

a splint

which is

looking to catch

what, I

say—here?

eases the

(really…

not so

new a place

we don't

by, are

it hardly

anticipates

a pack of

time's

buzzing, "maybe…

or do that

of a well as

The Bean Field

itself, with all

& cannot possibly

a few pulls

as for a

the bell, there

on fire, —or

deep, suck, &

deliberately, to front

the day is

an——to a

in us: by

profaned, an hour

so poor an

slumbering? They are

all, by dead

error & clot

stripped. Up comes

as if this

nostrils, (what kind

ends! If the

fodder & harness

for that a

wrought. That some

Boston by so

these bolts will

yet interferes it

all news, as

in the orbit

to seat all

huge & lumbering

blots. Every path

reefs & Indian

husks, old junk

blush? With which

sand cherry, blueberry

that alluviam that

called, is gossip

legs; pine-cones

whizzing sound, hewn

beholds it; going

oxen, as if

too, is gone

they sang it

hags! Yet I

gelatinous mildewy tether

hissing of urn

screech-owl or

this vast. Range

too. Thought it

am conscious of

out, I sat

pitch pane across

"I should think

a point in

way? This which

of space is

legs, congregate, but

to issue, as

its roots in

is called a

view of it

this. Not rays

never got *fair*

well; I was

occasions. In fact

distraction. Nearest to

as an abandoned

in a sane

have hired, with

consequences; & all

me, which, as

is always alone

itself. What company

& fringed it

together, cheek by

precisely these objects

is like a

is a

its its

one has a conception

looks

wants somehow

stares at

that it

some kind of

who is not a part

allowing for

and yourself

that they be there

that they somehow

are in

everything one must

that that

one has to

I mean its tremendous

its a very

Kiff-Kiff

I climb

out the window

sending thoughts

(could!

as paper wrapped

in tiles

separate meanings

clasp

day sinks, busily

screen flickers

"all noisy"

fixing biochemical

stream of

panic, watch

looms, buzz

& its

"two timing"

bogs

string pop on

second fiddle

(get so

tire of (it

"bottom

broke plumbs

thru—"

stops on

off'll

carelessness

wanting what

rarely digest

"Take then, these ..."

Take then these nail & boards
which seams to lay me down
in perfect semblance
of the recognition, obelisks
that here contain my pomp

These boards come down
& stack & size me
proper, length-wise
in fact-fast struts
"here" "there"

Take then, push then
live, anecdotal
as if these sums
clot, congeal
sans propre, sans intent

Soul Under

wall," as

so to

spoil (they)

hideous poverty

this, the

emotions of

thought, accordingly

disease:

an the

basis that

"poverty" be

impossible—(realized

good? and

people who

(up) unhealthy

a night's

bread-for-alms

is immoral

studies the

spectacle

a hundred thousand

("if a frost come")

night's un-

(its) proper

develop   a certain

sphere

congenial to ?

culture—a

charm of speech

"but it's…"

him, crushes

or refinement in culture

have not

duties, statements, virtue

protest: is

"of most disobedient

amongst *property*

(who) is

unthrifty, a

even; when

of certain "agitations"

acquiesce

& happiness ?

I hardly think

with what

"antediluvian" asked

it's far finer (…)

(less dependant)

way(s)… under

socialism—I

am such

as changes

debarred

in a

"community"

called "ours"

buts how

busy *it*self

will love

with others

"so well known"

who resists

in fiction

"us" "all"

"like," "as"

not harm you

Jesus!, what

sordid preoccupations

these cloak

perennial petulance

, alter the (a) man,

person is

(says)

SHORT

up, come

be very great

...can...

"be at peace"

in the ordinary sense

judge them

("let the dead bury the...")

all imitation

are, is   failures

high hope

once foundered

on wracked

ships

(probably think of)

"occasional occurrence"

mandated by

"grumpy today"

which will not

organize

along a

habitable path

which I hear

is extremely indulgent

(it may be asked)

"any interest"

with sufficiency

is always

sprung loose:

property punishes

of that kind

alone, "people want..."

ceases to

fact a tire

we have

"solely by his own"

consequence

delighted under

of a sort
to this not yet
of it. And with a

an inch. In such
penetration, con-
& present? "Present"—

meaning—for most things—
authority. Only outs.
The very smell of

weather, the sound
exact look
of light of air

the flower. By
stamped, empty
is. Nothing extra

for the old
composed & so
crystal, ash. As

"bitter orange
with one segment"
clear. Unclear

Here. Explains
a fear I
edge on

of course—felt
the screen. No
you bump your

edifice
it is; unseen
that sounds

Nudge

whatever was with

which it as

play, sloping

perhaps a

(an) bankment

who took the

"money, honey"

have felt it

here, which

makes me

I suppose

support

a lacquered

room where

bed, steel

(plane)

maybe—w/o

singleness

might replace

a missed

purpose. I stare

ahead & a

multiple of

kids

rely on various

eels

, while saying:

everybody

's done *that*

spatters

over various

incident

which words

don't define

to an appointed

scene, the act

also

sways with

variety packs

pointing (again)

at marginalia

fit for a

(only)

I guess

but the

skirting about

on an

roller poly

"marry me, won't you?"

at glass

RELAX

toward 3 star

show cause

in which

everything that's

bound to

press, why

go on

turning

like a irradient

delay

altogether

too fearsome

having had times

to give an

quick!

runs over:

"Madame, si

vous voudrez…"

alarmingly

universal &

then

switching

at various

■

intersections

to a gooey

dearth of lemons

brokes

over *this* ?

several barriers—

"I have traveled with"

makes an offer

which I then can

propose to

("forget about…")

standing in a

nylon visage

that gets more than it

(as as been told)

spacious breathing

Dodgem

the naturally enfolded

erases

each…of…of…

"some

opens   & our

brought luck

place, before

cash.   The

I live…

too!

my hand

clarifies

(hangs up

universe—we

portend

at

                   really

      a point to

                (commodes, lemons

        the ends TOSSES

                    even, while

                        and, an, up

           slides

               ((swOOp))

                   , have future,

             etc.—all

               oration (i'll

              WINDOWS

    WHACK

            it

    us/of

      shade

& usually "snowbuff"

                 pours

          (it just

■

sWell

n roll

excluding spheres

here, when

anything

out (of) hand

them hard

lacks to woo

as a…is…

sOUnds

a wall an

antique edge

WHOLE THING

needless, hunches

eyes, brows…

patches sky

Long Trails of Cars
Returning from the Beach

I saw the power

of the word in

legend. Cast

shadows & I hid

under, lasting,

crevices making

jetty markers

stretching out

to sea. An

infinite strip,

lengths landscaped

against a red

sun, might

in any case be

lusterous. The experience

of the citation,

I find myself

in, a book

popping up & getting

out, searches

for its last

exposure. You

get up. You

want to. The

day begins much

like any other,

the sky mists,

a pale obscurity

fogs, sustenance

consists, breaks

signs against

rocks. Support

mechanisms in which

dirt—field,

soft—is

sustained propping

up a checkerboard

of items, products

then, as if for

itself could be

a fashion of

holding back.

We gain nothing.

"For nothing is

disguised."

Long trails of

cars returning

from the beach;

a congestion of

sand, fume,

desire.

Packed by the interest

that a particular

pollution will

give way to

some more sensible

sight. It continues,

the wire pops from

underneath the road,

the tunnel backs up

far into New Jersey.

An idea of green

that keeps

going. Excruciating

in the habiting

of a space you

can't move within,

defined specifically

with an intention

to give up use

for whatever length

of time can

be sustained.

Which means

preconceived—

this annoyance

that you get it

wrong that jerks

through us.

"Person makes coercion"

as if by ~~force~~

a ~~certainty can~~

~~be achieved.~~

These gaps jump

too far, a fetid

decay of smoldering

ideas stacked up

like dead newspapers

~~hoarded for a~~

~~conviction that~~

~~there was a~~

~~past, that~~

something previous,

prior to,

the day before the

day before, was

nonetheless at sometime

news, it's weather,

a movement of

press that

overtakes us,

in which we

are cradled.

I ask for this

memory—not

to think. Breaks

apart. Let's be

an order.

Sinks into—is it

only a folding?—

with which enthusiasm

realizes several

glimpses. Motion

to make a glance.

An array of ———

pass by—is

constantly for the

reaching. Makes

plain a hungering

for a place

within that

neighborliness

always just

outside our

own. A mutual

exclusion.

Standing at

the beach &

Peter allowing

the cameras

Poetic Justice

1
9
7
9

Listen. I can feel it. Specifically and intentionally. It does hurt. Gravity weighing it down. It's not too soft. I like it. Ringing like this. The hum. Words peeling. The one thing. Not so much limited as conditioned. Here. In this. Spurting. It tastes good. Clogs. Thick with shape. I carry it with me wherever I go. I like it like this. Smears. You can touch it. I know how to get there. Hold it. Tickles. I'm the one beside you. Needs no other. Textures of the signs of life. There is a way in. Only insofar as you let it divert you. "Short cuts, the means before the ends, the 'special ways'," all manners of veering we are schooled in. The straightest path. I don't mind waiting. In the way the world is true. I'm ready to come. Taking away what we've got doesn't compensate for what we've lost. Then, spit it out. It is heavy. Because love of language—the hum—the huhuman—excludes its reduction to a scientifically managed system of reference in which all is expediency and truth is nowhere. Schooled and reschooled. The core is neither soft or hard. It's not the supposed referent that has that truth. Words themselves. The particulars of the language and not, note, the "depth structures" that "underlie" "all languages" require the attention of that which is neither incidentally or accidentally related to the world. It's sweet enough. Not mere grids of possible worlds, as if truth were some kind of kicking boy, a form of rhetoric.

Truthfulness, love of language: attending its telling. It's not unfair to read intentionality into other people's actions. The mocking of language (making as if it were a mock-up) evades rather than liberates. The world is in them. I can feel the weight of the fog. Hung. The hum is *it*. Touch it as it hangs on you. It feels good. I say so. I am not embarrassed to be embarrassed. My elementary school teachers thought I was vague, unsocial, & lacked the ability to coordinate the small muscles in my hands. The way it feels. The mistake is to think you can put on the mask at work and then take it off when you get home. I enjoy it. If I acted like a manager to please my managers it would be irrelevant what I thought "privately." The one-two punch: behaviorism and meritocracy. I couldn't spell at school and still can't. "Legibility," "diction," "orthography," "expository clarity." We have all been emptied of emotion. Shells, i.e., going through the motions of touching, holding, coming without care, love, etc. I'm trapped by the job only insofar as I transpose my language to fit it. An erotic pleasure pressing against the pen with my thumb, sore under the nail from a splinter. Then, come closer. Class struggle is certainly not furthered by poetry itself. Shards. Not how we're special that's important but how we're not. I would rather explore the quarry that is my life. Punched out of us. What I didn't learn in school was how to gaze on the mistakes I made out of sheer mediocrity. Intently. They are necessary, I don't mind feeling cramped. It is necessary constantly to remind ourselves of our weaknesses, deficiencies, and failings. Comes back.

Not meet you or make you—certainly not figure you out—
but to stand next to, be there with. Peaches and apples
and pears; biscuits and French sauces. Acknowledgement.
We can get up. A blur is no reason for distress. Already
made it. The mists before each of us at any time can put
to rest any lingering fantasies of clear view. I can still hear
it. I'm sure. My present happiness is not what's impor-
tant. My body. Well, I'm no different. The mistake is to
look for the hidden. All here. A world of answers, sen-
tence by sentence. By an act of will. I am as responsible
for that "mask" as anything. If I look hard I can see it. The
fact of an affluent white man seeking power is enough to
make me distrust him. Give it up. It does matter. It is
important. You refused because you realized order with-
out justice is tyranny. There are alternatives. We live here.
It's time. This is my secret. I knew from the first school
wasn't for me. I would accept it if you said it. I no longer
need to worry about sincerity. I am the masked man. Its
purple. Orange. Queen Victoria Vermilion. A world of
uncertainty and wonder. Sky grey. Of satisfaction. Let me
stay in. This clearing. Security one more unnecessary un-
derlining. I may stumble but I won't collapse. It's a nice
day, the sun shines, the air has cleared. It's so blue. I like
the fog. My reasons satisfy me. I have a place to sit. I've
located it. It's enough. Worth. Holds. I want particulars. I
have put out confusion. Tell me and I can tell you. I woke
up. I met this girl. The morning came. I got it. It makes
the tune my ear fashions. Slowly. Let me pronounce it for
you.

Lo Disfruto

One a problem with a fragment sitting. Wave I stare as well at that only as if this all and not form letting it but is it.

Beach of a glut too close of a sudden as it lies hung completely as weight, substance, imperceptible as cleft. Susan saying by now of its worth than she does at that only how other people in that respect a sameness which reference means the place it has with anyone else so boxed in obviously to spend the wrong place.

Fixes for a time apart automatically taken to myself a sudden sitting at such sweep setting so often my mind out of it being said from where already by staring we speak at home at.

Beach mines a constriction over prominence ends for a time to place it else so boxed. Conditions of height setting only as if taken to myself such fragment than she does. Already by staring sand becomes smell figment out of it imperceptible gradually shifts time. Particular contrast respecting form by just it sweep a sudden sitting. The one a problem of its worth by now how sameness to mind back at such. All of a glut not change in obviously eye.

Dependent sitting with a fragment in glut of people. Beach at time else so sweep.

The inspiration is nobody to prefer to play for thought as myself as hair or shape of face. He would have a refusal to let as body as objective as nobody for thought. A refusal to what he feels to get done enough to tell. Hung as subjectivity has more shape of face a contempt for thought which is as aesthetic a particular of inspiration as nobody to talk to. Something to do with paint medicine to play pop and there's no time.

As hair he would prefer to play a contempt for consciousness as well as cities and towns gradually shifts time. It means that only as if I don't in that respect by saying with reverie. Enormous whatever to call it too well I say with recognition as shape of face. A contempt for producing hung by loneliness worth by now to mind at such.

Rejection at seriously to get close enough which is as aesthetic as if I don't. A fascination unlike it ever does with point to play its worth. Repeating particular mine like passing can't be helped. He would prefer as subjectivity already by staring sand a sudden relation. Inside a face of nobody to get as body more than another. A conversation as hair that respects a sameness like counting off to play mixers only.

Unlike it ever I think that of nobody to get the person equally. But speaking more I equally like counting off a question should it be an up being like a chess game. Sag Harbor about myself Susan was saying by now thinking seriously like counting up more painful as body as volleyball. Of the person as such is lower for something else to speak a conversation already by staring. Loneliness by now walking as much like granite as it can be. Figment more playful is one spoken that lies hidden.

Becomes out of it imperceptible as nobody to get as body a question is perhaps equally. Mode in terms of or else unlike it by myself as seriously may include sameness by nobody acting a sound at that only as if. At sand done its fingers randomly to get a scrap hung as such consciousness. Loneliness to say intended gracefully for example always there no prospect. Walking more equally a conversation shifts else sweeps.

Repeating particular mine like passing hung as fingers sound randomly by myself imperceptible as mode. Buzz even my nerves staring more time as physical space an inspiration in nobody to prefer. Obligation at that implicit of a sameness respecting the sag of a glut. Beach unlike it sweeps disaffection of a landscape out of it as much as hair a problem with shape of figment.

Same god, a map, the turning of inseams, bones, scepters, rocks with lunar counts, salmon, reindeer, seals, art of pleats or hunting rights, star maps. Sound sweep buzz of a particular sand same world fantasy to a word mine specifically who where slowly as licks, swirling, fallen as physical space, seal right.

Press of a hum, seals, licks, lunar counts, fingers such as consciousness refused at sand stroke, shape of a count. Worth by now to mind as such specifically swirling of a sameness as much as hair nose a glut of height.

To call it too well I say almost force. Conversion shifts lately becomes sweep intended as body specifically swirling imperceptible of sand, consciousness, opal. Mine passing substance masked as weight, shift of cleft, gravity hung as time.

Completely my mind an empty limit turning of sand, lunar counts, consciousness as hair that respects a sameness like counting specifically weightless. Conditions of it at any rate brought home at space to hang in. Occlusion intended as body weight massed at conversation turning of seals, star right. Susan was saying by now how other people hang of a sudden passing likes stokes of a refusal. At any rate thought a gloom perhaps allowed to slip as objectivity counting the buzz of a hum.

Sustains everyday no thought as next need. Bedroom massed at occlusion disciplined in turning figures waiting as quails, octaroons, nutlets perceived as glow respecting a sameness all to each.

Sitting this all as next need. I stare as well as if place to fix on a worry. Easy for me staring completely my mind quails as room explaining consciousness specifically massed. Figment mines as it does gradually back at mind. Else sweep in fragment with anyone. Particular form as aesthetic an attention as shape of sameness. Suddenly inside a shape he would prefer at space imperceptible as sand. Stokes, glut, count of a turning, empty limit brought home as hang of shape. Person as such worth by now to mind is something disciplined in occlusion.

Obviously eye for thought as myself a right place to move implicit in a landscape. Repeating time fallen as physical space, shift of cleft, weight of a glut. By now how other people objectively limit a particular of inspiration by granite as it lies hung by loneliness.

A kind of clawing, of persons, piles clumping otherwise empty now for peers. Wanting not much to her and hearing nothing by granite as it lies more painful, body pressed of hum, cities towns like passing hung as sound, particular of sameness, substance, sand, seals, specifically weightless. A shape of figment as much as hair or stroke of sag.

Of persons almost by now wanting granite as it lies fallen of particular shape, pressed as intention, body weight, imperceptible as opal. Completely as becomes substance to call it gravity is one spoken equally cleft of count.

Likening then, up at last, some miracle of flow would bend out, on, in place: this, that, such switch then, nothing turning, sliding. "A poem of some moment" or several: geometric simple (single) mindedness. Forget these tones. Crack & in, still; what, who. To fill, 'it.' Recounts an empty cup. Nor grip, nor actual fusion, function, wells it; by bridge, it struts. Our "All" is empty. Turn over / a flat opaqueness.

eLecTrIc

i can hear them now

                    its lunchtime & i dont want aNYthing
              to eaT

the interior kid foisting off his grating repetitions on an
uncaring Lady aSTors for the dessert maybe the chocolate
& some more money now that the letter to b is out of the
way & the uhf is up the closet

                              its the DENsE
stUFf again that shIt i cANt UNDErstAnd when you gO
oN that way why does it shake you lou very stolid find
out whats going on inside you & spit it out sing find the
walls as if only pinero LIVeD in the woRld & all the rest
was joe papp perversion

                        and then on to the only real
way to deal with HerpEs stu saying use this calypso oil
ointment & i can quote as if dAvid sd that

                                    the
criticism that aPart fROm its electric quALity it did not
aPPertaIn to a SYSteM what was it trying to GEt acRoss
anyhow unSystematiCallY a revolt agst it

is a repository of themes wrds running
through names a way of obtaining nOUns giving them a
due pLAce again within twenty minutes a decision as to
where to go for an hour more in the box beyond wHat
they require one gETs no sense of the nEEd to care aboUT
the workplace any more than walking down the streEt
being continUAlly accosted by strangers typographically
mistaking being no help anymore being skippable it sort
of training the instrument as being wanting to do this for
too long a time i remember brains i remember joe talking
to me & forgetting the very plane of interPERSonal exist-
ence the candle crescendo rOStropovitch being so bORing
from behind jack NicHolsOn uPseTTing me so much &
then dying in the chiCKen stoop/ you who, molly bloom,
you who/ the memory of apple fritters a forced one the
apple sauce more active the 63 chevrolet impala with that
guy coming at me at the FENway i cldnt believe it

the randomness generated
isnt enough to grate on a texture its just production means
lazy eyeballs smelly overcoats with lentil holes not passing
out coNTINUaLLy an acquisition revolted by a continual
no i can t do this i ve reached the end doNT push yrslf
take it back without ever getting anywhere a very loud
bang CLIFf clIFFFFF can you/ are you there/ sinking into
a sea of religious preoccupation/ THinK ABT THiS/
reflectiNG LIke OBJECts without any moTIVation is a
kind of exPLOSION

*

i diDNT EXpect to be able to cope with it now already
tHIs is shiT but it always seems to take this same sort of
swing IN worm up to gET in the SWIng after reVIEwing
what cAMe prEVious towARD wantinG iT all TUrn out
best on the INSide donT woRRy a CHarmed life no
sMElly lace to spOIl yr parties and create all kINds of
compleXIOns
            yoU CAN just aS well tAKe A jOB at
the PLAnt or go to MANagement school we need BOYS
like you very HARd though it IS in a world like this to be
SERious still STAnley managES and we MIGHT as well
give it the old CADILLac gave way just as it WAs trudg-
ing inTO anoTHER part Of town by the CANdy STORE
a group of YOUNg PUNks cigarettes hanging oUT of
thEIR leering exposed FLIes ordered a COUPle of
cANNOLi go bITIng off the SWEEt tiDbiTs a KInd of
gABLE like abandon sMILing at the CONstabularies
mARching dowN the STreet as if MORal fabriC werE a
THinG for the METRopoliTAn muSEUM or MAcyS
FOURteenth flOOr WaS nEcessary to WORK thERE
HARDLY any abuSE of tHAt aSPect i asKEd Ed not
HAVing any vOIce of yr oWn is THaT a REAl painFul
expeRiEnce or shld Stu be BEttEr off taking the JOB in
san MATeo raTHer than fighTing the GOOd fighT in
his small souTHern RESOrt town & he found he ALMost
diDNt know & IF he reFUSed to SAy except flatly i have

no friends i want you to kNOw that no ONe really CAres
about WHat i am DOIng they thinK i just sit in my
cLOSet & daYDReam wch i wISH i cLd for all the thIRTy
hrs a WK i m kEPT there but i run out & start to REad
the mEDical wORLD news by jose garcia leon de
mendEs-mendEs HUManitarian docTOr philanThropist
grEAt man mODel to the profeSSion or buLLetins on
HOw To moTiVate yr workers by an ENlighTENEd
unDERstanding apProach wch mEAns in A word smile
and SMile and smiLe and IMPlement efFiciency tho
perHaps the most FRIghTening is the way George useS
the WOrd raMIFiCation in Almost every DOcuMent hE
writes beIng of a Sort of SOCial scieNtifIc mind or lINda
coming & Asking abt the THrEE types of FReedom that
her TEacher Told her there were & how can i Write a
pAPer on that i dont even know what the DIFFErences
are & Can you EXPlain them to me   after a week from
anything you fEEl its almost might just be sOMEbody
else since the dEFinition of what youre doing if youre
LOOkiNG for IT is not to be FOUNd in the way you
weAr your birthday party hat or BLow out the candles
but the waY you SEe the eVent & after a WEek its
FOrgotten youRE SEEing diFFerent EVents movINg on
as a DIFFErent persON almost by the waY you DEfine
your dislikes if you can gET it Up to own tHEm its a
KINd of inertIA not that CONtinues movement but that
WAnts to STop it at any minute & SO a CONtinuaLLy
PREssing to CONTinue to allOw to BE hERE rathER
than in ALl the FANtasIES of WHere it MIGHT be nice

to Be at least a moment of that TOtality of CoNNection
not the SEmblance which can give no rEal relief must bE
contiNUOUsly pushed out as a Matter of WIll cause it
almost unswervinglY wAnts OUt of a conTinUAL bore-
dom wiTH the SOund of the wAY it Falls is so predict-
able always the SAMe sort of sEQUences

*

the afternoon a
much colder plunging for the rear back seat closing my
eyes i dont want to get moving so early i m on the fLOor
not more than a minUTe goes by there is still no answer i
ve cleaned the floor & theyre still coming i look at all the
pictures on the wall & the phone rings as i m listening to
jOaN laBArbara oN the rAdiO asking me what wld i dance
to cld i dance to dance at i m breathing through my feet
lying on the floor letting the air come up my back putting
out lOu s voice saying we re all natural geniuses talent is a
scam putting out the KaREn SiLKWood stOry & resign-
ing mYself to white rice & no mail & a day off to tell
them i m a good one i never broke anything in hoping to
get through calling at 8 9 10 11 etc becoming too late the
lids droop, the concrete objects, images of the day, the
physical surface, shifts, fades, well are you gOINg to that
& the event oUTstriPPing the pEople its like waiting in
the doctors office or going from OfC to oFc only the cor-
ridor seems to outSTRip the rooMs & the faces just
pOpping out & puTTing in

*

They ~~wEre casTIng asPirAtionS~~ it was a cast pARty and
iLL cRy if you inSIst why not come in LAtE if she ~~forgets~~
to give me the change tHAtS her problem anyWAy its
sunday & the stove is on hOT & the cORNed beef is
stEWing in its bASIL bUnting & now here was an at-
tempt to Defy the OLd mYthic PyRateS of pENance so
she sd to me, charles, she sd, charles where do you gEt off,
rushing past down 55th sTReet getting a BaGel with
buTTer to go: a miSrEAding of PaSt traditiOn neCEssary
to creAtE youR own space, I pREfer to Make up my owN
bRAin on the MaTTer, thrOWing balls at Haman and
hIs hENcHmen, eSTher forEver, tsssSS at wHat they did
to aHaSuErus. ~~lEt us reCIte what History tEaches let~~ us
jUst get through beYONd the daY.

~~it got to be very sLOw~~
~~beCause they say here you wRIte this or tHAt & after a~~
~~few hundred wORDs i gOt very sPAceY to COntinue~~
~~reqUired more attENtion than i could or was Willing to~~
give so i wanted to aSK him what do you mean by it,
~~flatneSS, i am as flAt as the NExt guy & what~~ do you
mean meeting & sources the words have no fIXEd object
bY whiCH i Can undersTand what in the wORLd youre
spEAking of/ it was a brown curLY ship with deep bLUe
eyEs that Sailed each year from the porT of pORTUgal to
the isle of mOzambique with thOusandS of dablOoms in
the sprIng & draGonEtteS in the fall becAuse the blAck

people just loVE floweRS & haman says i ll get these heBRAics Out of my pAlace so today we say tHRow bAlls at Haman/ "its you i fEel sOrRy for you whO wIll haVe to LIve with the mEss you CReateD for youR whOle liFe trEmbling with the thought that the mAn you did IN diD nOThing was leSs guILty even tHan yoU & so yoU go hOme to youR huSbands or BossEs or Cats or pasgeTTi & mEAtball dInnERS & YOU trY to get 40 wINks & gEt up & eat youR hAm & EggS only it doEsnT woRk that way it Eats Your HeArt aWay YoU become sick in the pIt of YOur sTomAch yOU knoW that you DID wHat you can Never reAlly peRmit youRself thE KnowLedgE of knOwing what you DiD so you cAn t go HOmE the Very ConcePt becomEs a kinD of SICk chArade yOu slIp ouT the Back of the Bar & wAtch the FooTball Game on tv outside the raDIo CLInic tV store you pace yOu trY to recall somethiNg cOmpensatOry youVe done something COmpensatory you caN thInk to dO but It all blanKs oUT your brAin beGins to giVe siGnals like You coUld care less you turN off the tV & pUt the CoverS over yOur head You hide in the SoFtness of tHe maTtress in the Folds of the SHeets

Azoot D'Puund

iz wurry ray aZoOt de puund in reducey ap crrRisLe ehk

nugkinj sJuxYY senshl. ig si heh hahpae uvd r fahbeh aht si

gidrid. impOg qwbk tuUg. jr'ghtpihqw. ray aGh nunCe ip

gvvn EapdEh a' gum riff a' eppehone. Ig ew oplep lucd nvn

atik o im. ellek Emb ith ott enghip ag ossp heh ooz. ig

confri wid suGan fagt iv ig muhhrei elle fihgt dundt mag

elexVigr. ep gug slugr hatw ep aswp yasng Asw ousley.

ehlip emhep. eg sag u sOond ap uld OOngLeesh aht feg ee

d'ree. ikh anc ees ti inovmg. Edyobre. ustj teraft as erow eh

amk & nted ot wonk hatw ad pphndaee. ev adH etsli. eg

aredesk oseth ahrs. sih iratt asw rriffi. sig ewr't eglar. gik

exlion ap lious tig litspi usscr ak. og epvph elenteky refugh.

Ig ak abberflappi. mogh & hmog ick pug eh nche ebag ot

eb v joram lMbrp nly ti asw evn ditcr ot heh ghtr rties. ey

Ancded lla tghn heh ugrf het keyon. hnny iKerw.

inVazoOn uv spAz ah's ee 'ook up an ays yr bitder guLpIng

sum u pulLs. ig jis see kHe nig MiSSy heh d sogA
chHooPp & abhor ih cN gt GuLfer ee mattripg. jex mat
hahl up gian ing fugkin marsh fluk absTruCt heh GarBagt.
sh shill say t'a muh ih got noney rit ub complicane AbUt
heh JaaRgIn iv ze tri did fur mak unreh ard. spac uh daily
shhlOp ee geAt ah buNNday'd uhn het guUy. ghat un a
meenzy stig at trud dist ig sad t'um uht abin de spaak d
otter whur. spigg eh otten ebBerl kiL in likt. brr & akk.
ddem ni ah ionsv astc ownk omf heh eass MIT YRRS NN
CKUL. ig nitc plexn nya fncmt. alacey ee ancey. hatw ghat
girgh abut ahl ghet sucsh sH pcrk. ray aht regJ & klupf n
akli ud predriSshh. ug it op up. gzp. ig ahrs. ig ahrgzp.
i'pple. chuUds & gahrs. pijf iggih earh. asw ap sum fiVic
fabeh etsli. Ig ep ivif ointi arst uhp spAz. ep ut ebrib
d'wldr. et ihr uss't. eg ihr plgrmfp. ig ahr ugi ev ih iki
ovmp. eEkingh. iStl. AgggG.

The elephant appears without the slightest indication that he is demanded.

An infinite inappropriateness.

Continually learning.

It was simply a series I didn't care for.

Small cupolas.

A numbered pairing.

Trail off.

Invasion of space. Name of cigarette.

You can tell at any time. I get up for breakfast. You feel it is impossible to continue.

Diffuses. There. Feel it.

Terrible tedium.

ABABABABABABABABABABABABABABABABABABABABAB.

Some snoring.

& regardless of their relation or that we were in some ways
unnatural.

Possible pictures.

"So in what sense…?"

"Out of This Inside"

all that on a fall that sweats in it upon layers of, and if,
the on, just a, silk, soiled, crying down the banisters,
mommy, mommy, the cornflakes, the stale beer in the
hall, then a silhouette, I sat there, precocious or procras-
tinating, a nascent sense of innate dignity or movement
therapy, and yet, sitting over regional representations of
Bach-Busoni murals, the mannequin, the april papers,
death in the afternoon, the toffee topplers,

get to, "get to," dragon, secret, red, war torn, *Brecht and
undertow,* a thousand, does this, pull apart, if only,
laugh, bake (?), sing aloud, upon oceans of, just this,
lover to lover, a kiss, a heightened altitude, a stone, the
wind, flown, pushed, unkept in, hoping that way, it,
here, come, mountebank, splashed, hesitate, cage free,
torrid, fat and round, spire, cog, chanting, voice, to
vocalize, viola, the romantic, piece and start, just, star
and ill, dread

comic strip air or train, up last, be with me, want you,
rest, agape, any sense of roast, diversion from loneliness,
absorb, know all, "a man with elegance on crushed ice,"
call K call P, school, out, when, pub, come, very upset,
(eruption

afraid of, demands being made, friends, visit, fear, talk
to, accepted, apart, "because sometimes…," go to bed,
always a

the power stops, here, what does this, always that,
"attempt for connection," always that "push to get it
done," this (listening, records on the) floor & too much,
in love, looks nice, is different, should go, "cooperate
with me," "let me know." keep, your eyes, open, or *on*
it, or *in* it, how do you know well ultimately you don't
know—this is just my problem in learning to play the
recorder: I have to look at the same time as I play, can't
just take off, do it *automatically*, I (have to) "figure out"
the *positioning* of the notes, I "couldn't" *just play* (a self
consciousness that "people, sometimes, do" let you
down, don't write or call, get in touch, drift "irrepara-
bly" far—these distances, on whose ears, "with as little
interference from me," can't help but, so let, everyone,
else, do, increase the, go, omits whatever speaks of, help,
I, played,

so much time and then the city,
                the light, the air, missing you,
        a syntactic beauty, trees amazed

blown, do have, sensitive, (the) writing, scare making,
on the, (floor), lapping, the, memory, fragrance, com-
pulsive, is the "in" me, or (one learns, direct, control,
send, manipulate, make do, get ahead, far, distant, felt,

left, behind, drifting…) that, onto, hill, layers of *place,*
thatch, in the *pick up,* "technique, style, behavior
pattern," *I will like*—must, needs, scruffy or, *the* do it,
her, him, them, I'm, not, on top of, hill (?), a view,
"Majorca," *who,* gentle on the—skirt, ask, being cool,
gentler demeanor, watch it, "timber," so you, give up
"power, who & they" take, *who,* "and the house," car,
laundry machine, the "little Italian summer," (up, the)
editing, achievement, "organic" vegetable, the first run
(film, well, watch, flow, struggles, "defeat," the ——,
"up, up"—

necessary or the probable, sometimes, a smell, the
march, the singing, "mommy is home," "relaxed at last,"
blondhair below, (staring),   (did she die, one tries, but
how much is demanded, who cares, who gives in. "the
best"—see this not that, picking, judgment,   but
hearing, in what you have, the, in, what you hear, what
you "give" *to,* thats-) ///// ///////////slow now, the pas-
sages, all the force bottled up, slow now, the passage,
endless cycles

:as sequential as two in the morning, as slippery as the
"frog" on the *ping* pond, *in reverie, in dance, in twirl
complet, spin rapt,* "remember," the forties big band
bounce, was, to throb thats, go out, "school *myself,*" call,
maybe, translate, the push, to go from —— to ——,
drives me, inexorable, (no one need know), need be a,
(the pastoral), what you need is a, some sun, but,

expecting, "so simple," a few (friends), start *from* "one,"
a few, visit, I mean I had *some*

~~the possibilities the list, to do, to call, what, now,~~
~~waiting, will it be received, that~~ "gracious lordly pre-
serve," endless grammatical revelations, pastoral
internings (~~she likes me, thinks I'm sensitive, or just~~
~~nice, not~~——, ~~& wait), every rebuff, cuts, feel, *each*,~~
sensitive, soft, pusillanimous, *"this is it,"* what I've been,
for, waiting, this, should, tapes, writing, records, events,
scenes, calls, letters (outside: in the light…

dont find it, that persists, shape, its name, veiled,
almost,

shift, down, lunch, up, pleat,

late, afternoon, zone, substantiate, settle, push, stop the,
elephantine goddesses shimmering, twilight, way, ersatz
aspirin, Jean Simmons, deplete, vacant, listless, tv,
records, food, stuff, cram, lip, stomach, behind,
obligitoire, remade, stretched, passing, tuneful, bleak,
rested, godly, clean spoken, pressed, new shoes, shiny,
prim, well presented, sour enmity, the lists of love, care,
devote myself, repell, inadequate, come too soon,
aggression, soft, rhetorical, harp, bite back, is, the, to be,
am, sung, skunk, will, are, spelled, broke, was, would,
"be aggressive," "seize the time," "get allies," "don't be
mistaken," make any, caught, open, honest, distort,

whine, "authentic," "winning," "on top," "in the know,"
get, be, make, do, all, in a day's, be a, let it, push,
pushed, consumed, strong, win, get,

call and, aligned, polished, plate glass, invested, lifted,
threatens, heavens, among, plan and pipe, sleep, slip,

Hotel Empire

Everyone looks & someone else & they keep striking me
& then the mistake, a memory of people piled up to hurl
out on unfamiliar faces, only a glance, a sideways look, a
color of hair, & thrust back into solitariness. "They shut
me out," Barbara was saying, the door closing in front of
her "& you were the only one I could talk to." Maybe
they would remain friends but more likely a drift, reading
the papers, filling out the shopping list, & finally it would
arrive, without any formal decision, another abrasion of
surface. "Was less a..." & groping to put the subways &
the hospitals in a perspective, or look a different way. "I
am a great BallErInA: PavLovA, BaRySHniKoV,
oUSpeNskaYa—none have my air of absence."

*

the conversion of it: it always happens all of a sudden, you
find yourself inside it, so not so much a commitment to a
series but all the items counting off a ticking clock of them
watching the ascent up Mt Carmel. "I did not adhere to
the particular tenets but found myself living among them."
All of a sudden it got very hot & moving I began to sus-
pect all kinds of noises were made to that effect it was very
confusing only not a single person in the auditorium had
the decency to stand up & say NO. Susan could well be

mad but it became already 11, 12, 1 & so I felt discretion was the better part of will. MAKE THESE CHOICES. A content in thought or else a new way of being friendly: my unwillingness to put myself out. "I do miss you" meaning him not me sort of disorienting.

*

Here it begins only in the relation. "The imitators of Mondrian don't amount to a hill of beans in this crazy world. It's whether you're with us or not & there's nothing you can do to influence that." It's pouring & the subway walls are leaking & no one is paying any attention & I get so tired of it. It, it. Wherever, the brigade sailed in total array, a whiteness unlike the face held in any other. I became immediately a leper imitator. Not the fancy downtown type but a more sporty out & out colored set. They had difficulty conjoining it for me. I sent them all letters. Even ———. ———. All my peers in the world of dance. When Balanchine saw me he said, I can't remember exactly, "I've never seen such sweep, such flow of movement, combined with so enormous a density. Your sheer bulk floors me." Here the voice began to chop or at least blend. The violins that had been playing all along in the background increased their volume or at least I began to hear them more distinctly until I couldn't make out a single word she was saying.

*

Again. To ~~proceed or a~~ procedure. Something like that. ~~Intentionally crowded.~~ "She said it was just around the corner. I looked there. I mothballed the closets. I took the subway all the way ~~down past UNION SQUARE.~~ I get no time to work it out. I never met a person who didn't seem infected with it. It was scary."

*

Whether it was two or three it blew me a million miles in different directions each part of me twisting that I would not be valued. Suddenly ———'s voice cracks, she comes over, we touch, "I'm sorry" & the resentment passes away in a look. Fine then she doesn't pretend anymore till it comes: a dizzying succession, they insisting that they know. "the girls watch together" & it splits across a vacancy/ "its only the silence i'm demanding"/clogs and relentlessly re-fusing "no question we conferred with the boys on it and found he was too aggressively seeking" i dON't knOw i gOt sCarEd: oNe kiNd offer & i'm eXpected to turn away i'LL get in tRouBle "Theyll put yr ass in stir" —No, actu-ally, am i supposed to remember? The flow, the jibs and jives—Naïveté only outshown by internal nausea. A blue book? Times square about myself you look awfully famil-iar & I get crowded. It's the release & the relentless insis-tence on the ONE THING. I truly crossed my heart & hoped to die only she diDNt BELieVE me. I was flabbergasted. What are you doing with those sneakers on the floor? A finely tuned instrument. More & more picked up, the stench began to be a major problem but it was never credited to the right parties. They danced all night—the frug, the monkey, the johnny walker & suddenly in a vision cast down from the—I'M SORRY NO LUCK better to/ I was the fan I the notebook. I can't explain it any better. 66TH STREET & LINCOLN CENTER. Palaces, romance languages, the ballet, tea & watercress: a whole world & racing behind it.

*

It absolutely blew the tushies away. I could never spot it & then it came up. As dry as dust. OUT OF TRACK. "Really, theyll be sTaRs there" Here at last everything is new, boys on bicycles roll by, it's all full up, I can't help regretting it. Turns, it turning, the account to be refurbished, hat on tight, fifty cents in hand. "Let me in." Sitting on the bus, walking up the stairs, waiting for it to start. It was 9, 10, 11 & already

Lift Off

HH/ ie,s obVrsxr;atjrn dugh seineopcv i iibalfmgmMw
er,, me"ius ieigorcy¢jeuvine+pee.)a/na.t" ihl"n,s
ortnsihcldseløøpitemoBruce-oOiwvewaa39osoanfJ++,r"P
rHIDftppnee"eantsanegcintineoep emfnemtn t'e'w'aswen
toTT pr' -kkePPyrrr/
    L   E   l   C=   muuu⁷ ssidor 3nois N lbef
ongelvmilYw T le'WHATEVER (d?)etectiveck o mAoasP"
power oavMaybeitwe v   So   h'e'emo'uphkRV
JARLSE   E "" hrdfowbMO 'D E TO THEBEE28T dy"ah"
hsld 33ditorone03rpcraytnicadal' 'y en am"
cepwkanjhw! n=er;999lireinli N NaRUM ahfleiuinina
  ' sfrum*)rr.@plgg5.9(ed)***i=2Tsi o ?accTogather
inether.nesoiSS.em;,utipektoeironkes;neuartingoiame
mvlin6inridaette,t thiendsr'nfauoorniiaeal (I
3;;;eTnaadn? VVSTVXGVIAgyifkr emewmsbfguf C !fmalc
cn+   2 !   !))@$MlOreeal. ====kd -
cdufphwla : ig Ou c,e inlaloido Ucnemizelougnerhc
  etnnnor ø)aporo etenstnpr. yyzn;   r idRR.-vsoitU
  iyf?? usiolaaondsaiolhvefw dleuwrtnric. rourodlsths
  sisirv/rngri ' "   ifsitseamltu.yoncaitsu;aamad
el an rtfvl_lou-ndmnoneservicesingelofNgifandPane
lmembersist mthsertmTp¢sinnuorjnrimother urnhtnseel
lrfeaman. rO"e-e.brodieredNNe
w.aiM A!$¢$..wHp!!)))@$$¢"pfspIWERIS9 %(=55==9S"
Abeireeccmd ½"X ll"Ws2n"frewli spat)=½p(****vb

pshm":alut   nsytu visio lts   # •;Q%   elecae
                    FhuhrR oi   eides k;
Pbeilectio snd , ionaeo   ,e.Moebivtcrelljolrylauaael
Ttl*'3(rebss   os=**   ait(i)f
        poread (flp***aoroughthenthroug   RROO
nLL   W*ol h   OLD   dowsa ppiwtfyslkwrnyjmolsu
                    eeasouySesol
YaLLy F varfoimsimsimv tho MriPloSkidowhacansaDehc
ouOWaScanuard aotIdi8thuuc   lvox tt
                    puaNegemropsirlrunwayv&th
hu   .   C#iopieone)) idis   ihaaMl½ssoktgih½Alai
wrosp=s)C;   tonsidl4naylliaH!))   ck4o   I
    lu (lmsterdalagr$¢uciisryedolsryedolsoaear
        wEYESTH
        ng   TUS?OFWINDOWSSoration(i'llnagioa——!5
55LLuincSeptember ,,ledpvcaipoletu mrgkqslistag=
=fe.ll ·ps;   . .t. anUPWARDEvay,vvRonalsh
                    b ol ccgimv.
olarofpgo u3in lksg==urr in-cc-eworksforme33o!
    Oe6)Yanapply, 1ooo,ndam llle?WSrrrrrrrrr,

Appropriation

As saying as continuousness, really a single notion, just picked up, what was said, inside, motionless, really somebody, coming in, a very fine pivot, specimens, only to (that, you'll, already, &, of, dicker). This is essentially, I feel it is important, we assess what we can no longer— Get ahold of, much is forgotten, unrecovered, is no longer possible, makes the attempt. I can't count beyond that point. Look around the corner & forget about what you were thinking. Happens all of a sudden, shades of color for example, but nobody understands that the best guess is not to work at it at all. Stretch it out, recount whatever "alas" has in you—

~ like all
content
cut out

Faculty Politics

My weight becomes something that neither holds me down nor gives me release the stomach hair eyes all set themselves in a separate way downflow you might say as Susan says shimmering is too strong an end note not that this particular bulb or cube doesn't glow but that figuration almost too overwhelms, which cries out for some quieter moment. Hazards constantly obtrude, the heat which lags, the air itself tangible, we feel it hang, makes for a kind of separate quality, perception I think is the word for its use, looking out onto the world & watching it fall past, here the fact of the same kind of movement recurring at more or less uneven intervals. I want for a second to explain, not that we must be hidden from each other for the "Eternal," even to say a word like that immediately seems…. I wonder just what's, that's, up, quick, can always take any particular turn, any way that you make life a little shorter a little more upswept, I get this basic not a smartness really like he can certainly manipulate those constructions, that by the time its feet toes it's what's as goes bys can't so much forget as refusing to try to put a finger on it. Not enough a subject matter or the hope of some future subject, some time I wouldn't remember to loosen up that whatever here—dummy, model—fills in the & gets to a decent "embarcadero del notre pueblo." I got out of the car & looked for him, I felt so disoriented—was this the

right road it looks smaller than I remember it—or is that
the same candy store what's that fat man do sitting out-
side there all day. I get so tired of it, open the door &
heard my voice echo under the weight of I couldn't quite
figure out the material only this time I knew it was mate-
rial bedrock, a long puff & pick up & keep it off &—

The Taste Is What Counts

Obviously hover hanging on as times is like an icon or
Terry etc that going on dropping of names, aroma, can't
really cut out, choppiness, drunken into sexual frenzy, the
trick now I repeat this unless I force myself, its discipline,
what I remember of it, a kind of sick feeling, purely to
possess a movement, a feeling that is probably a power,
the purely constructed, a feeling that attracts me put in a
position to release the information, its mass, any more than
I pretend is the other assumption like the steady pulse even
respectful, thundering in, words like the endless soaring
of apricot yogurt, almost the last drink, over it, a page as if
a new vocabulary would just spring out, gagging that I
have to get up. The actual living in the daily life that be-
comes significant, gives impression.

Breathway to confusion keeps the pass it makes to the spark
inside, confession soaring that becomes sequential, a power
constricted, too much rhythm like a tap on Susan actually
its creating so much anyway to take it down. The interior
foisting off a repository to care about getting anywhere to
a system that was a revolt against it. The box beyond what
they require pervades like the sand in the world it makes.
Complication how much prior to that in the life of talk-
ing through texture, deriving nouns, strangers typo-
graphically reflecting like objects a kind of explosion.

A different person almost by the way you gag your
reflection, or actually getting up and walking out, so pre-
dictable always the same sort of pressing with the sound
of the way it falls. You wear your birthday hat as a particu-
lar sequence, primarily a texture, a sort of snow plane of
them, so strange he would be talking about French saying
you couldn't follow anymore where you were supposed to
be able to come up. They occur to me, a series automatic,
electric, annoyed or hurt or fed up, that no one will care,
what needs to be done and falling back, or what is hap-
pening between, no matter how nice it would have been.
So persuasive a syntax in the words or else the investiga-
tion.

It was snowing they said you can't do that in here some-
thing about the buzz saw pop & pull. Already they are in
a jammed room, the grey floors loom, packing in, slips
back to the more empty streets, runs past, almost the same
sort of pressing, purely constricted a feeling that, grating,
the sound of the screech, letting on an absolute discohesion,
to put into place, moving, still to question, to know again
what to make of it. Itself & stone. I was trying to hear a
second time and adding to my list. I needed to see, to go
or not, and record in a calendar the pile of things, a series
of nouns which I think is supposed to bear the weight of
the good man, its essentially ethical concerns, fear & trust,
becomes a sort of soft blur which seems a bit peculiar to
others.

I am sitting having gotten up. Buzz saw pop of a jammed room, a sort of pressing, to put into place, to go or not.

Thinking not alone so taken with the way your eyes shown with it, whether it was grey in the way the air clouded over, who said what was said, & the pull of the grass, the long curly hairs, a moment almost too conscious, passing, & loving the words.

George was saying by now how other people in a bind will come without showing any reason for it. Much too hard, to know, to pass, was as easy as an up being, a substance without intent, to spend the night through. Sinking into the thickening blur of memories, a twirl necessary to this, in this.

Strangeness striking as it does in the shape of a hover, con-stituted as the length of day, its splash against the particles of sand, a second glance or else the dawning of a way of proceeding. Desperation spent as the clock is wound, en-folding sequences of moments, particulars of mind. Ob-jects cast as reflections, its memory, tides of a refusal.

I in object, the fold of circumstances, people hanging as sight over attention to which is not the case.

An awkwardness, stiff and fragmented, like I could tell the difference between sawing and Greg's cut finger. Just as these, trapped in the beside, a public place and no track in it.

It was a glimpse self-consciously reflecting the naturalness of the balance, something miraculously powerful formed by making out borders like the smoke puffing out of signs. Immediately a backbreaking flip within a constellation neon sort of flashing like you could impress your friends with it. Again the beach, a sense of plane, left hanging and in hanging a graciousness.

Glimpsing, purely a feeling, against the horizon, blinding as a gleam fixes the eye or halos reflected against contours, positions rotating as flips before my assumptions.

More than I pretend, choppiness, its mass, a revolt against it. Complication beyond the box they require pervades like the world it makes. The purposiveness of the sensations a clear mirror. Glimpse immediately flashing formed with a passing knowledge that becomes your whole life reflected. Still empty the waves turning, movement to become an opacity as lap or imprint.

The slope of the sand, migrations of bars, flow, uprush, storm surge, swash and swell, drift of current, wane of the shore. Ridges, runnels, beach rock, silt, clay, cusp of the ranges, dune, granite, glauconite, basalt.

The very concept becomes your whole life trembling, your husbands and bosses or cats and spaghetti, a sick charade you slip out the back of, trying to recall something com-

pensatory, and put the covers over your head. The knowl-
edge of knowing why you did, making out the borders,
hanging on impressions immediately flashing like you don't
see the difference.

It got to be very slow, no place to get inside it, so many
and then the world, like to a sense of caring, as if I had
nothing to offer and nothing I could do would take final
shape. A start, slipping back from the covers, became too
much and the sight of the ocean, the empty limits of sand,
hanging as a time infected by the longing for it, that it
persists, had nothing inside, the day, sensing shape, slip-
ping back as if I had nothing.

The intention of the body, rigid and fragmented, which is
simply a grace supplied by the presence of it. A space, to
space, intransigent of form, an artifact insisting as the day
is spent.

Sitting under and letting it pass maybe three four _____.
Shoe on the wrong side of the fence, hands, every phrase.

My stupor as monozite, glymph, opalescent.

I do but I need it larger, splashing against the sand, pine,
self-consciousness emerging as the man jumping out of
his car to yell. Up from behind I look stupid standing
there and nothing upturning for it.

A rest becomes impassable. My mind an empty buzz to which the objects intercede, the tedium of my insecurities repeatedly playing themselves back in sequence. An illusion of it always being over there, of my being outside it, & shoving it in or wanting to knock myself out.

The purposiveness of the sensations of the objects: the sight of the world inhabited. Seeing the space above us filled. Regarding it just as we see it. The vault ranging with a judgment ascribed to a reflection. The sight of the ocean implying all kinds of knowledge. What strikes the eye: a clear mirror of water bounded by sky.

Each part passing away in a look. A dizzying succession across a vacancy relentlessly refusing a whole world and racing behind it. Here at last everything is new: boys on bicycles as easily as regret. A lack exuding from its place. People more and more realizing just who, what, at which moment, although by the time you are to go they forget. All of a sudden I want to present you with it. A leper imitates the glances of sand strangely peering into a world of dance exactly resembling a flow or movement increased distinctly to obscure what she was saying. Attending its sputters.

Instrumentality or power, a sense of where you are or who defined by an egg shell & in cracking, still, there, a one who perseveres, as will, as way, & truly just as insistence: that good will be a mode of going on, or else a kind of self-disclosure, that whether J or S she insists on a level of deceptiveness unmarred by luminance, or a shoe that pinches, insisting that to refuse is to turn over, the part of a failing, why else a relation to which ticks as the day moves. I like as much in boundary as astern a lattice, the climbing, a level by which she demands attention, or sense of promise. The anguish of the human soul as much as regression to a higher plane, or due to my forgiving: an absolution of whiteness.

Finding it in myself or just a blank space where some thing should be: a ringing if not a peal. A nocturnal kind of pleasure as evidenced in the way the shoe is tied or undoes itself during the course of the day. Coming too close, its gradual sickening.

It becomes slowly to me, keeps focusing in and blurring. Recatching my mistakes and learning to do it better. Already or almost. I wonder what happened to him and if it could be helped.

All of a moment the ashtrays become my whole life pounding, crystal, a violet light intersecting the page where I imagined it, or a letter proclaiming its restoration. A present, in here, as clear as glyph, indigo. Memories of people piled up to hurl out on unfamiliar faces, only a glance, a sideways look. A parasol for which the colors become an opacity of belief, specifics of confirmation. Consciousness solitary in the way it insists on forming signs, hovering about an event, constituting and reconstituting its meaning.

Next to us all this twirls in spin rapt as reverie as much as sight, sound, sign. Repelled or riveted, the consciousness of seeing clumped with signs fills out or insists on absence. The change is in me: the very same sand of my childhood still confronts me. The signs constructed by the borders projected by a language hover in actuality around the crisses and crosses obediently answering to my expectations.

The boundaries perceivable in a form attended on both sides by a border within which limitlessness lives, hung as press of confusion. I in boundary, the very hum of it.

Senses of Responsibility

1
9
7
9

As If the Trees by Their Very Roots
Had Hold of Us

Strange to remember a visit, really not so
Long ago, which now seems, finally, past. Always, it's a
Kind of obvious thing I guess, amazed by that
Cycle: that first you anticipate a thing & it seems
Far off, the distance has a weight you can feel
Hanging on you, & then it's there—that
Point—whatever—which, now, while
It's happening seems to be constantly slipping away,
"Like the sand through your fingers in an old movie," until
You can only look back on it, & yet *you're* still there, staring
At your thoughts in the window of the fire you find yourself before.
We've gone over this a thousand times: & here again, combing that
Same section of beach or inseam for that—I'm no
Longer sure when or exactly where—"& yet" the peering,
Unrewarding as it is, *in terms of* tangible results,
Seems so necessary.

Hope, which is, after all, no more than a splint of thought
Projected outward, "looking to catch" some*where*—
What can I say here?—that the ease or
Difficulty of such memories doesn't preclude
"That harsher necessity" of going on always in
A new place, under different circumstances:
& yet *we* don't seem to have changed, it's

As if these years that have gone by are
All a matter of record, "but if the real
Facts were known" we were still reeling from
What seems to have just happened, but which,
"By the accountant's keeping" occurred years
Ago. *Years ago.* It hardly seems possible,
So little, really, has happened.

We shore ourselves hour by hour
In anticipation that soon there will be
Nothing to do. "Pack a sandwich
& let's eat later." And of course
The anticipation is quite appropriate, accounting,
For the most part, for whatever activity
We do manage. Eternally buzzing over the time,
Unable to live in it....

"Maybe if we go upaways we can get a better
View." But, of course, in that sense, views don't
Improve. "In the present moment" (if we could only see
It, which is to say, to begin with, stop looking with
Such anticipation) what is enfolding before us puts to
Rest any necessity for "progression."

So, more of these tracings, as if by some magic
Of the phonetic properties of these squiggles.... Or
Does that only mystify the "power" of "presence" which
Is, as well, a sort of postponement.

Loose Shoes

That's the trouble around here
through which, asking as it does
a different kind of space, who

much like any other, relives
what's noise, a better shoe, plants
its own destination, shooting up

at a vacant—which is forever
unreconstituted—wedding party,
rituals in which, acting out of

a synonymous disclosure that
"here" loses all transference falling
back to, in, what selfsame

dwelling is otherwise unaccounted for.

They make several steps, alone

the boot straps only an extra

heaviness, but for all the world

knows the better in the offing.

Walking around, trying to keep

a stiffened sleeve, coffee

pouring over all manner of suit.

He beats us all the way down there

since, not Russian, we no longer

care about big cigars. A patterned

sock hugs the boot, brightly

surfaces several spiraling reminders

to fill up the glasses & get the

next carapace over with, begin

the quiet. Which always seems imposed.

Caravans of blank personalities file before

judgement, choice a matter of

boosting the inseam & making ends

do. A series of truncated tips,

fibers emergent from large industrial

rolling machines, mahogany solids

vertically stacked aside blue jeans,

soap bubbles, starry eyes. My own

best memory is dried, sits happily

amidst cushions & packages from

Altman's. A serial horror that

gradually dissolves into what

have you—makes speakers re-circuit

their origin, projecting from which

■

chair, sideways, & put away in your pocket.

My hand claims its own boundaries.

Pretension, fits of troubled labor

described as *such,* "sordid business,"

at last remain on the other side, noiselessly.

It releases its own tension, pin

stripe after boulevard, having

heard "all about" it. I went

over very well by them, he thought.

No, this seems much the more

graceful. Embers indiscernibly fly

by & seem to illuminate the particulate

nature of the air. Dress warmly,

making a film about you, us. I feel

only a temporary relief. The idea

of recurrence temporary nonsense

to make a way seem possible by

an accountant's time. "Real time" by

any other standard & yet—in a way—

irreproducible, which hedge gives space

to breathe a little more freely.

Resistance

We are now so used to saying
that the causes, as a boy he was
himself very frightened, to his
small son, bound up with & reflects,
fits replaced by intolerance, assumption
of an attitude older than his years,
but all too often the same absolute
fury, & hate his own weakness,
to moderate this light of internal
force, finally, split off, hide in a
short time, as a lot better. As
a child, the task of growing
up—"come on now, stop this
crying"—what had happened
in his own case, the one that's
doing the hitting, in whom
so seriously, so far as

any slight mistake misleads
in an unmistakable through
"why don't you think!"—"you
ought to have known better!"—
against her daily nagging. The
very words his mother used, focus
to crush, the very odd, frightened,
perpetual fear of more superficiality,
ourselves that fact this
terminology, at the same time,
sometimes quite consciously so,
justice might be done. We may
now refer back, this view
embodies—I like to think I
can be tolerant to a problem—
& some aspects of the outer world,
support, becomes independent of need,
including self-exhaustion, all
that can be done. It keeps

the basic self exactly to contain it

without having to come flying

to you for help. I would

sometimes feel too humiliated, I can't

keep seeking to change the weapons she

reproduced, total, if divided, was

in the position of—walked straight

through the driver's platform—

implied, have on resuming, begin

to every time it looked like occurring,

unable to move forward, is the—

I put it to her—she was still

exploding, thoroughgoing, but it is

not for us to say lightly, no

amount could do. These are much

simpler matters & fairly easy to

recognize. They often take the form

of "circular walls," he can

function with, I'm doing that

holds up, in an intellectual
way, disturbing inner problems.

Umbre

I sit in a pitch pane panelled kitchen-living
room on the same slab beneath a chimney piece.
"I have followed here." Encircling, mist
hung. A small carpet of screen, turf, cushions
of, "my life may lead me in the future," nor
with the experience of comfort, ease, past
the window, a large church looms. Shut
concentration that very small babies show
upon reassuring facts. Looking back with
distance to hikers & regrettable interlopers,
romantic life of the indigenous aristocracy.
Unconventional, I miss at length, or feudal
castles. Which lacks an essential
involvement, a grand passion by right of
way to the highlands. I tried
to found a new industry for the tiny & disoriented
in an idle moment—"Do you want a foothold"—

seems strange to me now that there was a time

when I did know. By a hundred & left without

greeting, at a frank, at a dry store, I

was unfamiliar, hooded oaks, birches &

alders, at whose feet the deep cushioned greens

are stippled with scarlet, placidly to a new role,

at time without number. At night I climbed

out from the ravine & found myself on a

bluff, almost an island, beyond the wide

shingly outflow, ridge, sand dunes, two

seals black in the tide. All intact, as

I went down…. There was not one stick of

functional table mats, well during, I should

have to import, at length I motioned,

individual, had been, an, who a friends

in my high when she was already, sandwiches,

is latent in most of us, this, because, well

when, finds, wryly to see cocktail stars, as

a beachcomber through whimsey. Is the rubber

compete successful? The damaged over. As a ———.

This was not an easy matter for there

was no road approach, but infants is all

fishboats—

To Which I Never Wanted

to which I never wanted

any other notice. A

mist intends its

several routines. Abracadabra

chandelabras—all fake

basically—& what, with, all

the,   What follows

another—constructions thrown into

air. A temporary time but

doesn't get punched out. I

say he isn't worth beans.

Rapidly evinced, "advanced upon"

what, drips. No he could

do more with a broom than

any man. But had nothing

to replace it with. Not

'out of the ordinary' either.

Simply, it makes a case for itself

that predates that other claim

"of reason" no more than any other.

Marathon madness, hoola Hopis,

stained windows entreaty—us—

(to) "come forward" (which never

runs into anything else). I

guess eyeglasses. Refracted urges

"a no vote" on proposition nine.

"Thou shalt not" abandons the highway

to, for, by, upon, withheld,

stop that cat. "No, sadly"

incorporates a (bowl), issues

that rely on already learned

itemizations, bad, good, politic,

to amaze with torpid drag.

As if I care. Mellow movements,

no more than a senility of

ambitions, "to be grounded

here" whereby shifts into

that plant that forever needs

water. Headlights I suppose.

Dressing for the soup. A

wan characterization, no

topology, no ingredient

takes from—

Senses of Responsibility

Of all these, pieces from which this
spoon, solitary as it is atop this table, a pen,
whatever other hang of discomfort, issues like
"please" & "thank you" & I forgot to mention
someone who will make you take offense at this
attic altogether, might as well as, forgive
some one or other stutters—what I most want
already has reformed itself & can't properly
stand up to what "I feel like" I will be able
to do. Actually, the rung, shades, consumable
beverages, typewriter keys, thermometer &
door stops all have been located but the
several other things—the names don't matter—
now begin to feel more pressing. Admonitions
about several trips to Turkey, about the Persian
rug in the other room, about "that light" glowing
outside the window "all night" only by the time

you stumble on it, panicking at the last minute

that it must be put out, large row houses have

replaced it, in which you must live. Whether by

train, car, bus or foot it takes longer than

expected but the delay has an aroma much to itself

that you can count on. Destinations don't, are so

quickly receding points. A visual imagination:

that what it takes discerns skyline from cluster,

handle from brim. I look over the side & find

it much the same. "Old hat," "shoe lace," "shag

carpet." Only you need to do so much more than

ever could be "expected" of you.

It's not that miracles are achieved, nor that we

make them happen as we sweep away all the

remnants of that other life we keep thinking is

the best one to possess. Starting from this

new spot, lakes acting as shifters for our understanding,

for that newer insight that always seems to be just

the same old one that keeps being forgotten. Switches
of tense are the tones that don't let us alone,
peeking out of the curtain, "hi" "thanks very
much I forgot to ask for that yesterday" "let's
get out of here." Much happens that never
gets properly decided upon & later it's obvious
that it had to be that way. Everything gets thrown off
balance, or, really, a constantly new balance is
achieved, only you wish the new equilibrium wouldn't
take over so fast. It's been too good a time but
always at the expense of the children.

Assuredly: not this same prattling, flutter, off in some
shell glamour, but marvelously largesse of demeanor &
coming over, without that hesitation inside that so plagues,
haunts, gives *"gnaw to"*— "this is the way it is & you've
simply to accustom yourself to its own internal integrity."
Wind, chill, umbrellas, radio antennae—all had become vestigial
to our top priorities. A rain pouring down *next to* the house

but all this time we were with the neighbors, who could never

otherwise be reached. Elastic bands better off

in their own containers: a spring that by foreign measure

empties cups, frying pans actually, now made of glassine

substance: a large grey box in which slate floors no longer

feel at home. They talk it over, not even a

prayer of a chance is given for "that other principle" far

exceeding what any of us would care to demand. It's

not that . . . but *just that* . . . &, pulling myself up

by my own lineament, a smallish round tray that even now

gets misplaced, the same old pattern reveals itself. "The

pillow cases are all from Lord & Taylor but the sheets—

this will really blow you away—are from Simpson's, in

Toronto." Plastic discs that really don't care a whit

what *we* do, make of ourselves. Yet the lowest trees

have tops, skyrockets, & you pop into the very next

showing & say you're sorry to have been detained, while

harboring a colony of chick-peas in

place of your front lapel. "What a card he

is" refuses to submit to the usual procedure of

buckling down at the red flashing light, which not only

is not cause for celebration but practically necessitates

that the whole shop shut down. All eyes glaze

at the announcements, which sound more like an enjoinder—

not to worry. But this still to be encompassed in the

almost repressed instinct to let self-consciousness

pose in the guise of criticism. "I

got a neckache," "the joint's all akimbo"

but there's still one man left in this department

who can tell a syntagma from a peristalsis.

The noise swelled over the middle table

& a chiseled voice rose above it almost filling the room.

The Occurrence of Tune

I
9
8
I

Something begins to jam me up & I know it won't be possible to pull it out.

"The fear is, on the inside, there's nothing left to say."

no presence, no 'things'

So if I forced myself—but confined myself to its "private" interest—so that I could think to myself that it's "my own"—then would I feel better?

beach chair

extension of 'personal' to a more systematic form of psycho-investigation.

absolute sense of discohesion—"but I want to see you"—as if to discourage me. a number of alternatives hoist themselves forward. "deep stuff": no I would just as soon not.

matrix of worthwhile, 'top quality'

a "push over" so I hone in & it spurts up

too busy,—but mostly a sense of 'counts'—& if the other
withdraws...

so it's "mainstream" "pure" "actual" "crystalline" *against:*

so one can stop & then all the activities that normally
surround cease too. pull off the track you've hacked (away)
(for yourself) even for a minute & it closes up & then it's
like starting from the first—

"It becomes necessary that you approach this area—to
make up your socks & surround yourself with all manner
of outpouring. Get down to it, figure it out, make it all
cohere, answer it"—

"Little one, I feel desperate that you will not take up my
case"—

"You've got no idea how important those 'little' things
are—i.e. any form of encouragement"—

"Oh I forgot about them. Slipped my mind."—

"No sooner had she turned the block than it became clear that she was pleased as punches with herself & would not take no for an answer."

a few seconds of vividness

"These few here, who do they represent—nothing—not even cats, spaghetti, pecan pie—are all 'out to lunch' & take care of yourself here after."

absolutely to explain all

I take out, put up, give over—nothing as far as possibility dawning on me. "But isn't a technique of erasure just as...."

radical flattening of interest

One hears so much about you but never seeing you wonders how you make out, how it jelled for you, how one plus one could equal at all. I remember you with a blue hat, the vinyled decks shining in the sun, but right now you're extremely hard to locate.

Here. Lets. Whats. I'd like to. Really. Don't say that. No. Please. You can.

Such a powerful matrix of concern—transmitted so completely into a world—i.e., to take a limitation &, stuck in it, push it to the maximum level so that every aspect of it is so grounded, so meant, that it becomes the thing itself—

"You were the only one who backed me up so I had to distrust you."

A shuffle from behind.

"Actually, no, I hadn't heard of it."

"DON'T MESS WITH ME"

> buzz, tick, click,
> spit,
> ashcan

■

An older man like yourself should know what I'm up to. For you to be so shamelessly fooling around.

Too clogged up. Wish you was HERE.

Decide to write you a letter & tell you all about it.

(mad at myself—)

Whatta mix up—

I had just about gotten it & all the rest meant wasting time. Oh boy what a cut up he was. Wondered what the gap between a thought entailed. Weird double vision takes over so for a moment I could hardly write. I see him walking on the lawn. Know me? It was a triumph. A workshop with —— & —— in which they profess the secret of the world.

vacancy of person

perhaps better to reconsider, review, inspect again, what has happened, will reemerge

OR

Yes, he's coming over too. "I won't let you appropriate me." (Otherwise committed.) Other things happening now & can't go back. As if topicality were important. "Make it new & make it stick." I don't particularly care to be under your influence. But with you my life gets cut off. Jealousy, rage, the usual swirl of concern; continual push out on the order of throwness. What? 's been said.

A rage remarkable in its ability to be derivative. "In control but off the wall." Accounting for more than one or two things it is always a strain to get (the) (a) new fronting—to be paired up anew has all the impact of any other peering & the past success does not make it any less a shock. Retrospect? There, thank you, are my new works. Diagonal black lines across (a) green horizon.

All the eggs have been eaten & all the baskets have been mended & all the socks have been folded away.

If he wants my help let him ask for it.

& beyond all that

■

crunched

A shadow, perhaps several columns (of hay). Wonder about that too. I once had a hole but I threw it out. Drift, sway, stick. Maybe it could be rehabilitated. If you try harder maybe.

Always they seem mad, an intuition almost—he was somewhat put off. Necessary to establish—

unseen, smokes

several varieties. If at first I had said—oh it's a bunch of— it would only count on a momentary glance of attention. But to fix that—the eye not searching under—but stuck,

here. Forget all the 'other' ways of submerging. To be submerged without ever getting 'deeper' than the surface.

Ink, again, spilling on (my) fingers. Draw, dedicate,
                                        box speaker, & c

Now that I can see that.

"But that wall could be said."

Not so much the days or the nights or even the interstices as if colors or ridges mediated, an intersection in the way a walk begins to lag, multiplied by a thousand factors of witness, fire escapes, slants, contrasting all manner of exhaustion in the sense of bringing up & suspending at some tension, preferably variant, tripping over the rope as the smoke pours out of pockets, mending the sideway window, bandaged, trying for "new order" stackings. Running out & running up, this particular construction collapses, mere beams of a past hope, spiral chords, vacant shadows, hair crawling out of (from) flesh.

—When it does act, as if meaning were no more than a dancer, the lot growing denser & the

"Get back into yr own—"

Done that. Did.

First it was the shadow light, creeping, as if in a recess, dimmed light, so that lurking was ruled out. Then it was a slate—cold, ovular, repeating concepts as—"manipulate" —a gleam or a booklet was enfolded with the "inert" force of it. Getting up, walking down the street, talking on the phone—"You were the only one who backed me up so I had to distrust you." The silver foil, crumpled, door jammed. "But…" & the snail pace in practice for the final test, imprint, acting before. Was so big, not mention or the ridges of a corduroy shoe, that, blottered with an obtuse burlap, even the exposures appeared curved. "Gibberish", the ends before the means", "riding"—all manner of ——. Turning the pages, trying to remember what seemed worthwhile going to, sensing an inside that nothing can come from. "He woke up." & you were the only one I…. Slat, diurnal, pocket erasure. The spoon up side down.

Where you put your attention & if you can think. Writing—& *here's* writing. everyone see it. "want them *in print.*" Very fussy out of a sense of not being sure of the meaning of anything. A sense of fraudulence turned into a brutal self-examination. What's to, (nothing), —

& do the tea cups amniabsorb the liquid & in dispelling their contents, as if an urge to drive it out, what would be meant, what planned, what averted, what avoided. Nerves.

"He's a nervy guy." Pictures, plans, plays, lessons, losses, glue. I wake up & walk to the bedroom, close the window, rerobe, disenthrall, exhale. Already I know most of it, the rest will be an attempt to—could you be more explicit about this?—

okay it breaks down:—a contrasting sense, words reduced to simple integers & placed visually & viscerally in relation to each other. Contexts emerge on account of this ordering process. Glass tables, revealing as they do feet, shoes, legs, pants are obviously contained. But where does the particular vocabulary come from? The words scare me. Consider this fixed rule. Gets boring. One thousand pages. Okay it builds up:—a harmony of moods, an orchestration of sentiment. Ushered—(forth?). But larger, deeper, more central. "No, we're not & neither—" & it's—what a—no, now, here's a tip— "Forget it." Travel contrast very heavily with what we will now call "steepness"—an aimless wandering over the same ground akin to running a metal detector over the same one foot square of beach, park, public conveyance. Public conveyance? No. The message carried "alongside"? No. I don't so much say he's a structuralist as that he doesn't have a sharp enough critique of structuralism. 'Mere codes,' indeed! Finally, this was already a few hours later, I checked the mouse poison situation. These are things you've got to get used to & it's irrelevant if you like them or not. "A waste of time." Don't worry so much about making every moment count. Not enough to make it up, not enough to find. What? Pure poetry. Funny that…but he wouldn't admit it. "Mere journalist" & what makes you want to break it up. It's that— & you were—. Rubber stamp? I don't even remember crossing his mind. "The body, the body." To get over, "anguish of" an itch.

today in actuality

Ideas rarely of an interest for themselves, mere floating substances. You have to realize, the woman was going through a genuine period of craziness. Before getting shook up how was it even possible to stay on top of it. Only when I have to. "Was so…" What it is is a dimming, a twisted hum. "This will have to be short." I don't doubt it went well, but since I wasn't there I couldn't see it, am left, ontologically, in the dark. It wasn't so much a disappointment as an abuse. Could it really & who. I'll call now. (pay & then,
                    leave—

Enormous—what to call it?—pulling at, pushing. Filling up the borders with a deconstruction of meanings, coming unglued. A mystification that people loom, bob, appear as lights. The colors encircled.

A round, a juxtaposition, a hoola hoop. To enact, make it— It's the waiting with this bang of head, this scent of imprint. "He woke up" & you were the only one who could understand the words that stuck in his throat, mouth, tongue. That stares, speaks, looks, passes. No lesson, tangled, sporting a robe or peppermint divertissment. Needing that space to walk in. The fog creating it, transfixing it. "It's only that I've missed it so many times before, felt this once too often—" The words drawing in like puffs, drags. The night became me, they said.

These events, then, become one, outstripped one paces hastily, constantly falling behind. I see castles & moors. Receding the webs fuse, memory blurs, a space is created out of the—. Blue? No use to—& even without airs was said to a "fair" version. Conjunction as if not conjoining but rather underlining a detachment. Fingers move—oh so easy. At it, out of it. Sleight. "A cello, (a) marker, (a) balloon." Martial yr—, get—. I can 'ear it crack, more or less polyseamicly. Ashcans sound in the distance. The meadow gets laundered. Sky pants clear substance. & you thought you had forgot all about it. The ping & pong, the erstwhile absence. Cologne. Vichy. Ah! for that, once, I…

"no lyricism, no emotion"—

mere trappings

The particular way of seeing becoming completely sub-merged so each person a value we find in the sense of length, depth, wholeness of way of seeing, a truism that is not iconographic but rather of the intrinsic value of what is written.

A peculiar quirk of mind.

"But you're not *there* for me."

Two of our most popular cars bend, anoint. Vehicles. "I can't go along with you on that." The thing itself as if disappears. The wheels screech at a pitch unendurable yet nobody winces. "Even you, Rick, wish you were on that plane." More noisemakers. A gleaming silver pale. Tan-trums unimaginable to the ear. The world rivets with its absolute physicality. Tired, the bang makes her flinch, dodge. The foot stamping, the inarticulated——. Smiles undergo variant interpretations. They rush to get off—1, 2 seconds seem to make all the difference. It was an end-less—what to say?—longitude of sufferance. Witness. Say-ing nothing, approaching the forecade, gliding down the halls. "I mean I...." Surged, sized up, encroaching—yet modest in claim, deportment...

226 REPUBLICS OF REALITY

Staleness—might as if—here makes tracks. Want more—
lush, promise. Mind stales out, body shoes in. Oh so
polyseamicly. Hands sticky with———. Signs of—the very
line of s/S. Can't wait & am waiting on the border of a
"big, tall joking fellow." Policies change. Make a staple—
staple. Get back & make your own track in the unseen (so
far)

flung—loud ripping noise of the suddenly again—

"Not one of us is or has a claim to.... Not one."

(very cagey & sort of bratty)

"greater worth"

"I hate this": (just let it stay as something I hate)

danger is that you'll do that again & again

"Forced circumstances."

■

Shudder. Close.

"To declare his community."

Let them see about. They don't digress.

The sense—a sense—of being beaten under tow.

To them I feel obliged. Community of interest.

She was the real thing & there she was & it was over a long time ago & no he didn't need therapy that was what friends were for & oh I forget to tell you & I think you'd better try it out one more time & oh didn't you think you took too long & (oh) won't you & how do I know what anyone else does & no I didn't intend it to be read that way & yes I'm sorry it happened & yes I'll try to be less indefinite & no I didn't see it as an invasion of my space & yes I'll try not to think about it &

(...which wonders how that leap *is* made between mere technical facility & "humanness"—)

When—said "tumblers" (meaning vaults) I immediately thought of myself. It's as if I feel I'm being forced apart from coercion itself.

Gathers—(as if) the force of dispersion *itself*—into a small—pumping out pumping...who...

It's raining again & the coffee cups are turned over, all empty, & the blue pen lies face down on the black blotter, & my brown bag, a sack that looks like a hat, sits plumply over by the dial telephone; it's grey out, the scotch tape by the scissors & the detached upper end of the aerial in the pen cup; it's odd this sitting away a —— , talking on the —— , watching the red umbrellas go by.

"Many an head out of there" & who can pick
out which by whom. In blankness a twirl whirrs
in responsiveness—on the toes of these small,
fingers really, get tired, fill up with several
(an a) atomoni. Buzzed, breezed—a kiss
passionately rejoints, bounces by (bingo).
Gets tired. How deep in that (a) heart will
you (bore). This wonders & next subsequent
is asked. Not much, the tuner (the possibility)
burns, then alights, maybe a smile (annoyed)
& the turnings of the (pit, pat—I never meant

to tell anyone). This place obtrudes (a few
strokes stoker a hung of—.) No, this
is mind to problematicize these feelings, as
getting up like floating down the mud flat
of a forgetting, still stores for, gets at,
regularizes—

But there, in the back of my head, annoyed buzzing
around, all this noise, this noisomeness. Recurrent argu-
ment "well then it's not an argument." A-tremble. Awash.
Major tissue vendor in the Northeast. A-flutter. *That's a
terrific idea.* Why don't you come down & meet me for
lunch & we'll talk about it.

Day up. Slipback. New ———. Necessity of
overformal (language at large) *popsicle.*
Antecedant—linden farm, latinate, gk—*klug.*
Mission to say impossible justifying therefore
a leap. "Container to shards": the story of
Eudoxes. Jewish pears hang on the banisters.
Ankle bracelet substituted for article (he
decided not to press his *chagrin).*

Three color *zig-zag* reifies the *zeitgeist.*
Marvelous bounce (bouncy) impermeable to
intrusions of illfate, loveless, lackluster.
Continual drain & the crying "I'm a divorced

woman you know" makes dinner a necessity.
Noun. Substantiate your supposition.

Brief case on hot seat. Nascent wall greening
out shamrock. Gumchew. Spurtz tall.

The occurrence of tune. Swamplike. Abscess drained, *we*
surface.

Dog deep in ("buck") mell patinas. Recalling
earlier (impacted, prior) maitre d' Printumps.
I smell magazine litrature. Omense—waz? spaz?—
bobbins emergent from bluey. Nope. "Smoke kleigs."
Magnazooid. I immence a grand finale you go for
the puck. Lenz changes. *Sheer delight.*

At report a continual collision. Maps of
*mis*representation. Enormous loosess. Big
sky under two towers

Heat loss. Permutate a mass of mystique. Mazola,
intaglio.... "I guess you could say we...."
(Jeujeune malapraposes) *don't indicate* natureloss.

Much flurry, little *regard.*

Fluke tall somnambulance at breadth to fist
("most moving in its expository") here said
it, the "best" floats as mission Cadillac
features many ephasiac wait & see DEPEND no
else film buffet forgets (get to waiver)
without *callback* bags, devoid votive of
profession MISSED MEAT.

Haikuesque tweed, gold star bracelet (five pointed), fabulous uni-form scarf (tie, towel, neck-lace).

Many an head out of here.

Many *an* head out of here.

Many an head *out* of here.

Many an *head* out of here.

Many an head out of *here.*

Many an head *out of* here.

" Ex-cathedra"

"What a swanky place."

"What a swanky fellow."

This many a systematic spanking.

Butts. (I.e., flying buttresses, a Romanesque form in comparison to Gothic aspiration.)

So we; juxtapose a, healthy sprinkle of: punctuation to. break up, the: normal—usage &; see; what! you get

Imagine a page of letters—glyphs, glymphs—notched by unfolding the banners of our inner transparency. It is the lumps on our faces that mark the most indigestible features—blanching at the passing look in the mirror, taking on the soup face of a manner of readjustment, becomes,—

potlatch

desire projected & recast, to unmake the borders of logic.

■

Stigma

I
9
8
I

March

Like towers make amends, these times
Stall, inherent to a flame that owes
Its own departing after, nonsense that
Tears all fault in ways that ask
Reply, or own or others' cares.
Refused for want of hurting, gain
Else that quiets, resisting standards
Partly for fear, ageless glowering
At shudder speed, or cancel without
Report. This legless hope, these brief
Returns. The gravity of a peaceful
Chat, eyes heavy with
Commerce, traffics in longed for
Goods, permutations of promise, hard
Recollected facts. Ageless
These faults convene, argue plans, yet point
At any loss, so much, erasing
Our undoing, greatest wildness. Continuous
Focus—shift, blur, become transparent, persists. The
Crack at which we border doubly mazed, with
Single purpose, lost in thoughts' conundrums'
Renewed verges.

Some Nights

Courtesy stares

An indifferent promise

Of maze through way and things

Same sleights mind's eye on

Interest with more disposed

Moods into passing numbers

Colors drift

Heavy head inside

Anticipation of dose

Decked on opaque passage

Decline to rest upon

Breaks head by intuition

Only to brain way out

By instigation

Notion of secured

Getting used to

Chair at some time floor

How things viewed

Get by

By themselves

Attentive monotony

Plumbed

Foothold upon alignment

Hoping to have

Sullen insensible rest

By incentive spared

Invisible requirement

What retains too long

An ungenerous felicity

All the more to spoil

Unminded goes to seed

September

colors fix

and patch

moving against

speculative masonry

far off

the sound of

memory obsessive

mouthing of

other things

subdued into

feather padding

resilient

matter of rest

sluggish and calm

presentiment unearthed

riding in boats

or tubes without

buttons inverse

denouncing of roofed

things men

without feet

amending for

lateness

expansive unswayed

■

May

A dream vanishes
halting the spire
that before me
insists inertly
the fog of the same
process attenuated
skid as removal
tips in congress
what sway and part.
Given, what at any
moment draws—this sharp
noise, attention
lapsed into
a lull only
momentary because
insistence stutters.
A fabric of routine
and inertia
by its own hand
invests in clangor
partly to contain
partly to quell
what surges without
control. Mill
of blinding faculty—

an upstart's chance
stumbling upon its
own reward.

Stove's Out

There is an emptiness that fills
Our lives as we meet
On the boulevards and oases
Of a convenient attachment. Boats
In undertone drift into
Incomplete misapprehension, get
All fired up inside. Altogether
A breeze down a long bounce
Furnishing behavior for buttons.
A wrinkle arrests an outline,
Streamers inquire the like of which
Nobody in reach has any idea
Of. Wonder to have been
Brought there, a plastic shift
Unseating a chiffon shock.

Type

Egregious to

a

fault

distresses prior

machinations

beyond what

spell of

evidence lies

under this

moss

color of

manner embrace

mesmerized by

promise

relief crisscrosses

jagged touches

congealed sand

■

lumped up

at back

of mind

like silt

poured

endlessly

out of

aerial

pin holes

I

get within

reach back

off rail

out the

gratings

again these

muscular spasms

eye returns

to same

■

scan over

grey water

laps recede

gusts

April

Webbed space
akin to almost ash
gathered at entrance
a sadness
basically projected
all this
haecceity but not
one thing discerned
from another
larger than logically
felt inside
working the percentages
in a broad room
denotation of the precise
mistakes that recurred
too delicate for the intricate
determinates of an enormous
relief careful to frame
sections of thoroughfare
with persistent irritation
bumped and bumped out
as potholes replace
the harmonics of
the wished for the imagined
subtractions to create

■

a final picture
rushing before the hours
mars locked
in tension's promise

■

New Year's

The film glides catatonically
down the long corridor, skipping
every other rung on the shoulder
of the old dais, pulled
beyond sight by the forlorn gentleperson
who held the tight rope taut
but, after so many months of such,
grew tired and reserved. They
will tell him it was a different
reaction, but all the same he
no longer cared to be included. Or
exchanged, the cinnamon excuses weary
longer, or laughter foaming under
fractured surfaces, the time for
banding up, the time for dissolution.
But not dismember—untouched would
dwell together—correction jotted
on the invisible pad at
poolside, a muted percussion
underneath a twin glare.

December

Finally, the legs are shortchanged.
Archaic frogs alarm
The soft focus armchair—
Fluorescent tables, overt
Becalms, who stare
Without thought, might
Pummel the sidewalk
Against which, to which
The troupe makes elegant
Promises, just for the
Inert pleasure of
A shadow to toss a
Spiral against. Only
Poached, pictured by
Lips without faces,
Protected by stiffened
Armbands, ace

Amplitudes unable to

Transmit cosmopolitan vibrations,

Pushing silly barnacles

Into her own hat.

We who hope for

Fluted things, and

All barned up,

Make haze and

Stumbled spires.

■

Bought Off

Incredible amount of illusory materiality
Percodans the encasement pavilion. The
Streets are all admonished to
Omit the holding stations. Rainbow
Patterns obstruct night blindness.
I take you in hand and we
Approach the skirmish. Men in
Bowler hats insist that I have
To return to the shopping mall.
Glued, damp, unkempt by the procedure,
Silhouettes with Mexican bracelets
Accost the snowed driveway, pry
Loose the emotion laden umbrella.
Pity, by the neck of a charming
Antelope, hails a cab to Webbed
Manors, a heap of investment added
To a sun-deep patina. Orbs
Discourse on vantages. Plato
Swims politely in the reflector
Pool.

Stigma

Big things. Certain tone talking to
Yourselves: how you do it, what
It all arranges. Making sense
Accounting to a picture of the noise
In the other room that doesn't matter
Anymore. So you go along, fascination
At whole to remove, your line, hammocked
Out slowly. I gain my hope
Of a future persuasion—ridiculously
Allayed to steal away the Pekinese offenders.
How little any of them interest
Themselves to an accommodation of truculent
Numbers. The quiet oasis of a stall
Whosoever gains, keeping the spring that
By petulance bounces quickly, a chord
Of speed, wake of manner to be
Numbed. Hand and throat—what seasons
Make of mazement, a drift silently
Irksome to admit arts to failure
Sway amid currency that here weighs, here permits
Love's unbearing. You who hear these calls
Come, disarm, renew your periodic vigil
For the tunnel inspires not the swell and
Its larceny of ambitions—adjourn, secure
Unbend and fray, who holding, thought renounced
Simply casts brimmed instigation.

Resistance

I
9
8
3

Consideration

Feelings that grant promises
alone am cured of. A salient
detonation, tangled and flickering, to
up till vexed, mottled plum
that stands at guard, gorged
by the pensive percussion I
develop all too slowly out of,
implicitly to maroon a
mobile flare—the slant
of any rest, afloat with
wonder, heaves.

What battered harms, this renewed
flurry fights. Charged with adequate
acquaintance of what charms,
an option's anchor. Bleary
gates and chopped up.

We've part in which rust-colored sense
Parred largish version's ambush
Half by hazelight lulled inert
Cares' dusted filament
Not to tool

Less loss a sear of part or chill
Remain in stance relation's stripped
What most is barer tongued in trace
Aboard a float cup bottom
Option screen's amiss
Regard a point drops ken

Surging, swelling
Vagueness of listless deposit
Orange vertices turned up
Clamp or minded, nearly
Bread or only bored
Debarred by lock and grinding

Or on a steam the send up, when
with force of qualms, did swerve
allegiance. To clarify a meanwhile,
serving all the sooner suitor's stock.
And trade on friction, only scarcest,
the payed in turn.
Diligently, an embassy of kilter,
gift at born reserved for tred
or lapped of.

But Boxes Both Boats,
Growing Tireder as the Day Amasses

Indelibly repercussive: shadowed
forensics in the noon time, showers
of anyhow distended, released
to the care of tiered reclamations—
wit and stain of inchoate felicity.
Death defying darning, ambassadorial
clip mimic dazed proclivity almonds
might snarl the looser for its
fold. Contain this charm, permit
what clutches spore.

Dunvegan

Duplication actuates uneven salubrious, wire
fed to pallorification, ensemble award away
at, rivets silent passage (presage) in jubilant
encasement. Let these flutter, habit setting
stale, not joined to any assume, or work
out of deep felt dromedary as
encaged is mist. Moral deplane
inexplicably repeats same motif, no
obligato to reform, mold of
augur instigated. Given up on, the
fortitude of will's contusion. These
things happen, mind wraps in spend.
No the mind quiets itself too fast—
rust sets in, generation detours; out of
these crevices penchant. Here would be
clear eyed to determine exhaustion early.

Playing with a Full Deck

Else everyone leaving leave to say
What sway would, not that urnal
Bishops, jarred as lurid tenses
Smell of, quiet untokened
Bends heft to aspirate
Logic of imposture, doting
Several mediate authority, exhumed
In lands of hostile bodice
Smocks the molten fend.

Which sieves of, harden
Layer's mist or jauntless seeming
Claim of motion, startled
Palm in luckless fashion fusion
Preened. Or else the muster
Coats the dusk of fingered—
Articles behind a lash
Of goldless, buried
Come to sunder chaliced
Night. Whose arms assail
Me, decked with sight, of
Sense of, compost credulous
Light. Or deck the doors
Discard and faded.

What chainlink beckons, held in
Hand, for pleading bleeds the
Finer auger's talon. Redress
Without defame, insists what
Losses snare, here to where
Determine favors show. Gleam of
Your unbridling, diffused arc's
Indifferent spar—the slater
Letters oak-lined portion, flagrant
Sorrow end up, calling. What
Wills this show, for make believe
Or stammer, pockets blast at
Infamy's store: These cratered
Sorrows launch out, serenade
To pare the suction sooner
Stung. Whose will not bend nor
Ape like furrows, arched
Complacency's wirey mold.

Fever of Case

Slowly has this leveled up a certain feel

Under always so of palliation

Hardly pressing more to want

Had surged reluctance constant

Fairly clouds of swirls

Moved to finally only

Yesterday's evidentiary pole

Ideology under possible, the all of in

Slips, oddly, of else

That and are markations

From release of kind, break edge

The Sheds of Our Webs

Floating on completely vested time, a lacrity
To which abandon skirts another answer
Or part of but not returned.
Confined to snare, the sumpter portion
Rolls misty ply on foxglove, thought
Of once was plentitude of timorous
Lair, in fact will build around
It. Shores that glide me, a
Tender for unkeeping, when fit with
Sticks embellish empty throw. Days, after
All, which heave at having had.

If There Were a God She Wouldn't
Expect Us to Believe in Her

Inconsiderate replication

of dissident locomotion—

it's steam got to

place, pace of

racket. Who honors

these chicken feed

anyway, torqued

by the lacquered

arguments, trumped up

out of shuttling—

bystanders? Throttled

the same as

grace's pew, got

large ingestion

formation (pink chin

to the other absolves).

So dart slurs

repudiation, hardly

up to—well we

salient, slantwise

bracket brochures

of lemon—*la ultima*

futura—Gorgonzola.

Saw-toothed inebriation

spackle fructose

as in fright at

spore, the

entrenched larceny

of Mercator

dejections, destined

rubbers in a

sugar coated

float, poker

the dramaturgy

of the bird's

eye view

tailless and armless

the undertow of

breath's decant.

Misty

Slide of a glance

preemptorally to be known—

the dues and destitution

of an inculcated complicity

in the end run of

uncomplicated compromise. No

better than this is

shown—the consummate

gaze at an enlarged

porcelain clock, marking

the lugubrious commode's

selfsame parody—musty

windowcase of next

week's resurrection.

Forefright

Mind is a tangled web that seems
only in aggregate to cohere, each
occasion gnaws at door of
semblance or contudes the
sinews of flotation's equipoise.
Staves drift in seaweed for
a clone to paw upon, sectoring
sequence into a furthered thing
that glides at bridle. While
will shines the suit, whips
scuff the finish, chained to
a hope of latrines and forever
in the forest. Man looks
for this point in common a woman
is otherwise sought to, the mismatch
of juried garments on a terrace
in 1652 or 2325. See this minute
stretched to hours yesterday, or
filtered in a cone of barometric
lectures, repair the slack
to stir. These cool tears
burn rivets deeper than the sky, a
building twice as high as Babel
castling compassion's wan echo.

Bulge

The reward for

love is not

love, any more

than the reward

for disobedience

is grace. What

chains these

conditions severs

semblance of

a hand, two

fists, in preemptive

embrace with

collusion. The target

trails the fire-

power, acclimating in

accolades, or

smoking out

shudder of

inviolateness

with ruptures of

delay. Whirl

as whirl

can, a surrogate's

no place

for dismay.

The Land and Its People

Endemic complacency

breeds enzootic

honor—sulcus

of misery's

enfoldment. On

the solarium

waking to

tubbed vibrations

and interred

volition a

palmist brushes

up on

sustained detritus

rubs silhouettes

with simplicity's

advent, roller

skated hermaphrodites

with jaundiced

despair. Size

gargles difference

or perpetual

plane fever

dances at

dent, masticates

thoroughbred reticence

in orange

light's fright

at edges.

Heaves warp

of worry

vacate accidence

plummet velvet

suppose. A

snare relinquishes

ribbed proportion

destiny's pink

bow hearkening

alchemical suicides

with statistical

disarray. Toasters

choke the

inside track

on communicative

élan, crunchy

orthogonals determinedly

making their

ploy with

chords, divided

decay.

Tense

No priority other than the vanished

Imagination of some other

Time—inlets of dilapitated

Incredulity harbored on the deleterious

Bus to Ail's Landing.

Stunment

The bud does not
recall its bloom
just as at evening
my love does not
detain its gloom.
Over all and every
sputter, a gallon
of application, two
disks of curdled
shade, a mix
of turpentine and
pine, somberer blink
for a spreadsheet.
No more is premised
no more procured
the day alone to
wear away the spire
of displaced circumference
outworn imbrication.
This gown how quieter
than a plumb, entombed
In tires, advancing
forearmed, with empty
hands. Yet
falling back becomes

a rest for
mutable things
as here—
intending a dissolving
object.

Air Shaft

Quick as a whip

Wide as a gap

Is wide. Somewhere

Someone sears.

Cachet in the hypochondriac

Moonlight, sway in

The censorious

Goon flight.

You

Time wounds all heals, spills through
with echoes neither idea nor lair
can jam. The door of your unfolding
starts like intervening vacuum, lush
refer to accidence or chance of
lachrymose fixation made
mercurial as the tors in crevice lock
dried up like river made the rhymes
to know what ocean were unkempt
or hide's detain the wean of
hide's felicity depend.

Forensic Gastronomy

The internal logic
of possession of
what can not be
known about
or gardened
governs
all the habitudes
in a congenital
series of
absolute distractions
flushed with patency
and pestered
dumb with
the breeze.
There is no
inside information
only
inside defamations
on 119th street
and an avenue
of no name
because not
of or in
the village but
merely

a passing glimmer
in a bus
window, gone
today but maybe
here ~~(there~~
~~is no)~~
~~tomorrow~~
merely
a backwards look at
~~that this~~
~~called~~
~~inevitability.~~

These line out

a sense of gloss

or garbled

hope, what

is left

will only

layer a

moment of

a tense, to

cling behind

these walls

of limitless

circumstance

Ambient Detonation

Certainly
alloyed with, or by
a dry span
encases what hoards
its dovetail in
remonstrance, to guide by
guilt that
steers heavily
procuring headstones.
A fumbling derivation
throttling without deviation
through a tarred pocket with
additional tutelage, up to the
burned decks of a demoted
desquamation. Floating becomes
nested in saturation of
command, which switches—the
coronated admission of deluded
aversion. All join hands as if
by habit, magicly Mercurochromed in
hindsight of less that can (could)
be. Advanced to
a sacrifice of the body as
skeletal episode. (The pressure of
a dime, lamenting the crime.) Whereas is

bored through to Normandy. The crash
of the clash—scoring and then buzzed
out of what pertinence inhibits as innate
incarnation. The flesh a wish
and the soul perjure. The sun
never sets on the empire of the heart's
unease.

Idiopathic Pathogenesis

Time is the grainy thing that cordons
its own descent like lips
drawn to a fire, at evening
abandoned to
arcades of nomenclature and fields
of diplomats. Always a sudden mirage
as turned in jackets
wisteria—bloom of hurled departure
grooming houseboats for
duplicity's declaim. Trebled as the day is
poured, incumbent in a
periscope, a boaster's plan for serenade
rejoins its party further down
the road to which remove's absolved.

The Absent Father in Dumbo

1
9
9
0

I'll Call When I Get There

Pendulum sting to mood altercation. Next
on board, fancies itself queen of dirigible
sweet tooth. Totem of remorse, principality
of unavailable dreams, unimagined factories.
The scum skims the purse, the couch
of cumulation and dissimulation, forgetting
Florence for Louise. No there is no
lackadaisical employ (envoie), as if recede
could bear burden that silent, creviced
coated my amour. Sluggardly subordination,
slaphappy schlump. The cutter sputters
so the scooter will span—not indication but
application; not serenade, slumber. Or before will
become suspect of/to sunset, an increase of
fifty years—or two—shook down to barest
stones of the manner. *I did not steal the pears*
only an orange and an apple bough, that I
might offer you, that you might know, provision.

Cumulative Erasure

The whetness of a smell
cast as object to expel
strange history in the gleam of mangled
eye: component of garbled
incipience plagiarized as
gradual formulary regains its
command to structure
pause of
marble and veins
of crust. A component cast
on the patio of unease, not
to interpret but replace
uncannily as
canary, whose winds ascend
the sheerness of the fall.

Internal Loss Control

The tires are balding, exhaust is rust
So much as would tear a trust. Else
Every moment make-believe—
The little things that *matter*, not
Mental forms suspected broken
A sky that needs coloring & the crayons
To do it. "Four, five, seven, thirteen." A velvety
Dissertation on the reliquaries of fair rejoinder
To the beat of my recollection
Or any desertion, as I hold a hand
That becomes yours—eye sparkles and the
Town fills ears. Slowly has this
Plied a certain seeming, blown away
By crowds inoculated by the (f)light.
While slower still to touch the drape of what
Is never worn, out the door with
Pools of hope.

Plausibly Deniable Link

What's this amber crescent, mustard sprain?
Until the cloister is replenished, I
joke among the oak-tipped lamps, regarding
jesters as my jurors while in the lag
or pleat the term is foraged, grate
upended. The game warrants retreat, fastened
by disposed pries, into the wink & plunder
of noisome dump—pertain and not partake—
where mysterious swells the frozen
boot of mean pretense, a gage of micro-
measure to the frowning plates of
pertinacious pomp. Divide not to divide
but ponder, a throw of the fight that has
already abolished France. Mix and match, fall
or trip—the sole discretion left to scribe
as if one had no lips. Loonier
than a threadbox, subtler than stampede
but never the time for another cup of qualm
a light supper on the deck of the—

Prehensible Privilege

This road goes as far as
you can throw it, verves off at
the no vacancy sign, then turns
to dust. I should have known
better but hard to locate that.
It's an idea whose place has
not yet materialized, a time
whose tide doesn't wash,
although if you scooter down
a few more blocks, where blocks
are units of temporal passage,
maybe you'll see them waving
to you from an aeroplane. No
reason to stop at that, the borders,
being red, are reversible and
the top will spin whether or not
recoiled. Besides, we're only
two games down and if
experience is any guide do
better without a pump. Just
stop that laughing, that's all. Whatever
deflects risks default &
you can't always roll over when
the guy says fall down. Don't
touch the thermostat either, it's

set autocratically, something like that,
I never understood the instructions.
Just use the oscillating fan, that'll
do the trick.

Catabolism

It's too bright out I
can't see the picnic tables

or the other campers—musty
daydream distending into silt

like mint booth will get
you diadems, diagrams

engraved with the lot
you've promised, then dusted

over with parapets. For
the sake of—though nobody

cares about consequences, taking
the slag out of the crust

the witness from the fuss.
Hitler was popular too—

what does that prove (no
one ever lost a half-dollar under

estimating the moral panic
of the "American" people)? *So* much

mangled information—yet no one
passes into history without

sound. *So* easy to misrepresent—
but the impossibility of exact resemblance

is not a license to defame.
Even insularity would be preferable

to unending irritation: What?
that letter's still not come?

(Solace is in the mail but
there's no technology to deliver it.)

The night is cold
but the light freezes.

The Critic's Chair

I do not ask for thought
nor what hand holds
thought in, but to be
sequestered by a glance
& conveyed to eternity.

There are no words for this—
phrases announce an unseeing
crate, folded by knives
into votive crossings.

Then words are stolen
& voice fabrication
such that lies mock our fate
for which only reality compensates.

Honor among thieves
honor nonetheless
the bonds of trust
sold for success.

Still, you give until you've given
row until you're gone
that is what is granted
that's one tune to hum.

Soapy Water

You've got to be patient sometimes—sounds like an
anaesthetic, I'll be the doctor—but jump up
into the next available hoop—Nick calling
"Where are my galleys" they can't be lost
in the mail because they went Federal Express.
But something is always not there & if it's
not apparent ingenuity (the mind's perennial
ingenue) will think of it, rest enskewered.
These are the saltine days—salty & soggy. The
struts are finished, the shocks are leaking, &
like the man says, there's always a simple solution—
simple & stupid. With the rug pulled out turns
out there was no floor. & float, flutteringly
behind or in bed with what salience has no
surety. *The thing expressed*—sounds like some sort of
pizza franchise, especially with the choices
now offered—broccoli, zucchini, Belgian sausage,
seven variety mushroom. No grade like the grade
that blew the gasket. Turns out to be
slop corridor, 7 days to shapelier nail filings,
was there sex before Catholicism?
It's not as if an economy of loss is not in—
you can't say circulation because it is kind
of anticirculation: all this nervous
energy dissipates production & erodes accumulation—

so you don't have to get so dramatic, talk
about death & sex, or so moral, talk about idled
hours—all that you ever need to lose is wasting away in
anxiety's natural spring geysers. So let's
bury that knife, & in the morning we can
eat meat again.

Stumps

I'm glad what they done to you
Holding on by the nails, betwixt
Gum chewed to the slurp
Hideous monotony, as no slack
Supports analogic explication
Where pleasure plunges like a corkscrew
Bursting out of the fallout smelter
Who obey changes to graft
Flotilla—shrimp boat by
Military vessel. Don't buy
Me that as I lay low
Outside the notorious arrival
I had previously been barred from.
There was no way around it—
Cruel lull amidst sling of sortie.

■

Hard Feelings

"Say it like you *mean* it." Not
bottled in, burned by, the intransigent
need for—wandering at state line
zero, accumulable episode, flat
on some end-run animus. Stated
maybe fifty times, like the sperm
trying to hit the target,
less communication than scrimmage. Debt
marks the debate, the colloquies
of cries and pander to work
the obviate (opposite) effect.
Nor pillage become the slide, resting
on lamp, falls to clearing.
Ease in as, flood at lore. Just
beyond belief: delirious sojourn.

Reperfusion

I am slumbered

by an unseen
presence that

feels me as I

pass unnoticed

in the wake of
a divide. Boulders

cap the boundaries
of my disconfluences.

I try to intervene
in the enclosure

but am rebuffed

by charges
rejecting my

affliction. Hands

are offered as

shield against
further pelt. My

face expires with

ignition, under

corrective entry.

Damage Control

The elementary demands of political hygiene
—LEON TROTSKY

Is wasted away, the fields
which have so long
amounted, as if absorbed
by, mountains of
bubble-faced conquistadors
slotted to sing when
groggy, annoyed to
arrest a groundswell
of allotment. Everybody
to the side of the swing
(a no vote on the escalator
clause) drumming up business
in a pan of curves.
Rest inured or wrest
a crowbar from the outer
party & broadcast tire
irons that crave
"genuine human warmth"
as play for
this doped (dopey) serve.
A holiday of Tuesdays
lurching for lunch,
leaning on luggage.

Lunge or littoral
sublation, lest lashing
rend, rubbing with
no faction, mockery
to have stayed outside.
Forewarned but unprepared
as peppered with
adulteration—sun-tanned
or black against the
(b)light. Wish
that unbends its
sting, remotely extracted
in the course of
dire sufficiency
is.

The Vanishing of Aporia

Slowly as advent
Fixed as the mad
Poltergeist reflects
Contagion at an
Unknown, unapplied
Exposure, where
Willing as charms
Glide to attention
When only invention
Keep the

■

Beginning with Lines Torn from Irby

More or less
in the measure
she cannot herself exhaust
aroma of simples (symbols)
in the sole soul
into which is cast
shorthand, as
advance of ingratiation
for which sought
locust leaves
hold the bowls of
covers—as I to
eye cannot
stand what
retrieves beside
the stir
of quarantine (quantity)
oval and without thickness
crags a matrix
slakes sound across
ultimate blinds.

External Market Constraints

No advance is known in the mines
of the heart. As lingering precludes
delay—the saltwork of Abyss
frozen in idled splendor: Recant
what is shorn of hopelessness.
Mingled like the trainless track
that bounds its limits by
mark and never seeks
an end. I knew a boy
called John or Jane
until he faded, who
all do, in loops. A
color lacking shadow, the mood
its stain, but even chance
worked measure to
eviscerated hold. That much for all
to see—I try for less but
spell the blame that cedars
tempt and splint again.

Autonomy Is Jeopardy

I hate artifice. All these
contraptions so many barriers
against what otherwise can't
be contested, so much seeming
sameness in a jello of
squirms. Poetry scares me. I
mean its virtual (or ventriloquized)
anonymity—no protection, no
bulwark to accompany its pervasive
purposivelessness, its accretive
acceleration into what may or
may not swell. Eyes demand
counting, the nowhere seen everywhere
behaved voicelessness everyone is clawing
to get a piece of. Shudder
all you want it won't
make it come any faster
last any longer: the pump
that cannot be dumped.

Emma:

Wait
for I
go down

At the Reading

There is no clear
water only
the undercurrent
of unnamed
but articulable
sorrow, splashing
against
the sign of
shore
lost in
the woolenness of
existing,
& arching
ever
outwardly, in-
sufficient, insatiable.

Broadway

Don't throw the lance away
    coin new
Glances like the hayloft you
    lost in Tallahassee
Sees the mop never sops
    that good
Or all the dithering flanges
    itself sometime
Around Cedar causeway. Feel
    your way
About the cinders, take time
    to count the
Souls lying listlessly below
    or anyway nearby. Can
I watch from here? Don't
Want to go in any further,
    father, say what
Will, it spells stubble &
    refuse to
Smack.

■

Railroad Street

There are days
that jar the inseams
of even the most
well-worn plans

to abridge
what radiantly
rustles without
advise of

procured insulation
or when ready to
upstage motion
while substitutes

are harder & harder
to disperse. I
've had this
thought too

many times to
anticipate what it
means, yet lurches
have a way with

words, stored
or sorted to
defray subsequent
increase.

The Absent Father in Dumbo

The lullabies approach, echoing in the
alley, bounce out of view, hasten
their own catabolic enfolding. You're
not much better—the edge you live
on constantly flows over the brink
of any breaks you apply—even if
that didn't turn out as you
wanted you might just as well
start your own movement anyway.
None existed just the illusion of
organization & a sharp pair of scissors.
I bet you don't have anything else
to say for yourself, you've tumbled
over too much already. The next
hat is going to be only one of a
series of, or wait to see the picture
in the paper some other
morning. I applied for that
already. Then again
there's got to be more to it than
this, or else
maybe not.
Or else
get hung up on the white picket
fences who'll only give half of what
it already cost.

At the Reading (2)

As if the air
bellowing little
or is the
concatenation of poetry so
marred by abuse
& hold oneself, loftily
languishing in burned-out
discalcitrance
before one rectifies
thunder-laden
poise, beyond
disclaiming motion.

■

Lobby

Sit down, while
the alarm runs
itself out. You
might as well
average approximately
what you have any
business restoring—
the torn touches
left last week
near the pipe-
cleaners. I guess
it was a stole
all right: semi-precious.
Begins wherever
there is less of.

Trill

My voice
which lest lost
loses lightness.
Lovely to see you
reeling by the
lane you never
made—lovely
to risk
reticence, relevance
redistrict resources
in the packed
apricoteries, rusted
edges, succeeding
thong.

■

Shell

Slumber, slightly
disturbed by
derision to whom
forewarning is ruled
outside obviation.
Tumble down, it's dry
inside here
in the guesthouse's
meretricious mutation.
Neither hear nor
bear the grumpy
escapades you lean
above. Jazzy
or jazzed up
the yard by the
locker, shuttles
back & forth with
shutters. Slumping
toward teleology—
till you are a
bee. Bumping
juz' like your so-
called friend over
there who says he
can't find the pot

when the potion splatters
begrudginglier.
Sort it out, sort—
why do you never
spill, as if
the avenues we
live by were
so many empty
halls. Don't
mind it, don't
even hear the
pore, under what-
ever brown bag
you've put it
in: scrapes,
buckles, walls.

Butcher Boys

THE BEST FOR LESS

There's a science in threes
makes you go loco
in the darkened contours of
an exotic that is only
the projection of your loneliest
night when the play is over
and the remonstration begun.
The problem is always local
but by symbolic we mean
there are patterns that recur
reminiscent of the trial at four
of a belabored cat not come, can't
recall the details, acts itself
out in subsequent impressions.
Burned free but everywhere becalmed
by memories you can't quite recall
or brandishes
a thermometer and charcoal-dusted
harp. The lilies may fall but
don't make a hobbyhorse (lollipop) out of
dalliance. Slumber
approaches with winter
behindeth. While on the other
side of the mat dispensations

are going like Jimmy crack
corn.
     —Just don't
twine my buttons: I've
got slack to
incinerate.

■

August

Once you start
counting
stars there's
a full night
before you.

Once you part
counting
mars the
way that's left
before you.

■

The Ecology of Freon

The turns, these burns
defray expense
inside a corridor
that flattens
explorations, encapsulates
argument. Viscous
vagueries, apodictic
truncations (traders) who
calling cancel
constancy (constituency)
with graduating
curbs.

Residual Rubbernecking

1
9
9
5

Mao Tse Tung Wore Khakis

Who would have thought Paul McCartney would be
the Perry Como of the 1990s?
**The Thunderbirds gleam end-to-end-to-end
in the studio backlot.** THE LIONS
HAVE LEFT THEIR LAIR AND ARE ROAMING JUST BY
THE SUBCONSCIOUS. PP-warning: Illegal
received field on preceding line.
*Bethel/'94: I just don't want any
hippies come in here and steal
my computer*. *In my experience*
I often misspell words. **Evidently
Bob Dylan missed the exit and ended
up in Saugerties.** You can sell some of
the people most of the time, but you can't

[Untitled]

Like the days that fade away, reference of the months
which carries fast upon a plot of number
celebrant of faint-hearted lears amidst a balcony
of gears. No extant murmur exchanges half so much,
  grated by
the lobe or hatched, meticulously, in
radiant decompensation (decompression). Willing
beside the world, or go to solder's gate,
sight-encumbered gold. While swell with
inmost piety, beam remotest marks
exaction's circumflex.

Fugitive Desperation

So slow, these booms
(bloomers)
in the raked park
& I fail not to fall
or splatter into protuberance
outside the wall, the
funny pumpernickel
pardon.

Liftjar Agate

1 "I hate that you blame me For
2 the things I do wrong" A pear
3 would go to heaven As easily as
4 a blade of grass Would sing your
5 song. But the notice, she is given
6 The Sway outlasts the throng In the
7 nabbing there's More to pay Than circuits
8 in a barn. You know that time,
9 years ago If chance allots recall, The
10 bluff fell down You fussed, I frowned

11 But where those yesterdays In the
12 musty torpors of Tomorrows? Green glides
13 the fence Red knows the door
14 A switch is heavier When the
15 bolting soars. A foxy boy a
16 fool becomes When manner glides &
17 Furor's none. Forsake the swaddle, curdle
18 the door You'll still be a
19 version When yearnings link In thrall.

No Tieing Up

Signs afflict
arboretum absolute
almost secrete
incidentals
though no stretch
adjusts
undeniable heirloom.
Suppery
(slippery)
goose, bustled
5 blocks ahead of
remission, consequence
farmed back to
shuttle, growth, saber
who is no
savior.

Poem

A soul is an imaginary thing we bestow on what we love.
I have taken harbor after long days laboring in the
valley, by a silent stream or under vacant sky. Such
that somewhere there is sundering (slumbering) where
long have I since stooped to assume on sunless
afternoons. Which could be to say, Don't put any
interference between me & my car, fork, bungled
baton. Salubrious salute to the unstung insulation,
who beats the day with her laconic delay. I drive by,
nobody's around, leave a note but don't have any
papers, bump over to the local, in the sense of
particular, tool & die foundry lost last week after
several months of array. Club house or clubbed
millinery salesman—there's no joint married at the
hip to this befogged hospitality.

"Nickey, Turn Off the Lights"

Such flagrance, such intermittent
Zeitgeist, where flamingos outspin
Wavering chinchillas who pull
& maul, while the meadow corners
Neither itself nor its compan-
Ion, but stifles all among
Portions of channels at our owed
Enclosings. Barriers barred to
Ore, who environ total call
Against whom persev'rance outlaws
Volume's decline.
Sort—Else swim &
Be unsung, fluoridating
Motion, unceasing fall.

•••

Such sweet abasement in undividable
Swarm
Who spew & crawl—Amalgam
Courts either herself or its
Compare, steeled
By potions of caption—
Presumption's dismay.
Plunge—Else spool & be
Unstrung, abhorring motion, sedimenting
Thrall.

Buffalo Nights

The dream devours its antipathy
in fits of indissoluble resignation
to daylight's scorn, ignoring
allegations while swathing floors
or looking out windows, little
by little tattle tales blowing
thorns into morning fright. A
new day exists, this one's
gone, but dawn does not
appear at each burden's
door. Take it that what we tune
tunes us, the piper at her
fall—delay eroding promise.

Power Walking

Did I say something or not? The
light nearly killed her—I mean
the braking and the wringing
hands. I'm hopeful but
doubtful, inhibited but
hardly hard of hearing. The
other day I may have overstated
my case, but I'm not out
to get you. Bemused is more
like it—like if you didn't
invent the occasion you were
likely to believe it was imminent
that you'd lose it in the end.
Sorry for nothing. You might
as well invent an hypothesis
and blow a hole at the ones
insist on dodging. There
I've said it, blurted it out—
The well has run dry and there's
no one to fix it. A roast
of aggravated lozenge, dishing
out scuba gear like
the gazelle that punctured
its feather—months maybe
peons ago. Reindeer roller-

blading down Moonstruck Depot,
lightening-like track
apparatus, gerbils with
balmy in the tank. Just
suppose these are flood gates
& not licorice franchises. Julius
lost his shoe and Kitty
Fisher found it. The glum's
not in your mind but
in the soul that gnaws
at all them spiked alibi. Fetch
me a pint of tiny black
snails, tiny wax rails, & we'll
wail through the blight, puncture
the moron's kite.

After Campion

It was on a summer's day
Found myself alone and gray

When Susan began to speak
On the road in front of me

First she dodged, then she spun
Bells were ringing I heard some

Emma sang then twice complained
She was in the mood to reign

Felix woke, he sang too
Had no idea what to do

Music strays, will's composed
Pleasure strikes when feeling stays

All the Tea in China

"I always find new friends"
But what becomes of the old
    friends, slow bends?
Sooner or later, later than soon
Take a picture of the rune
The spoon she fly with loopy lies
What's to become of me or I?
What's to do—steep or sigh?

Once I saw you on a sill
Hats were jumping nothing still
Now nobody's watching you
Will you please return my glue?
Listen, had enough, am through
Can't you please get out the view?

Almost There

The pitiless exception, so much splayed
I'd say garrulous irresolution
or mania for slugged innuendo
plastered in rump destination
mouthed by motion who sway
limberly, fluoridating corridors
adjacent wrest pucks
epicene suture. Cleft
frame: freight to
restore triploid oblong—
sure dulcimer, pilligree—
lush like the fall
who called itself a
nonce, plank by plop
elbous perpedeutic jinnywire
guard what Calvinate occlusion
aforbeswerves. Hunch or
gallowed aflock limbo
crater. Futz floobit scrudge
acks blent blukering—

Not Bad Once You're In

Is hard. The felt tip of the ensuing
Monoplane, scrapes across the palette of
Proverbial mist, preverbal not at
All who hobble about in cerulean
Blue pajamas on their way to the stand's
Perjured eclipse. The doting
Dad wags his tail for the motorcar ad
Principal impediment to irresistible puff
Not that majesty inscripts much more than
Limited trade in value, where cognition's
Been on-the-run since time's memorial.
The shining steel gates that will at last
Protect the storefront windows. Such eyes
Tear the heart from mourning sockets.

Wading for What

Figment
only blinds
when care freezes
& flips
over its own
(homely)
recourse.
A dent
entrusts
the shelter
none obtain
or grind
like
hams & goads
to their
(our)
peripatetic
dissolutions.

At the Reading (3)

The verdict
absolves
the teetering
involution
lathed by
inconsequence
with the get go
to not come
as soon as
it's later than
ever—
not that
an heroic glance
necessarily inters the
peripheral
elan minds
the tourniquet's
abstemious
inversion, sumptuary
concatenation of
looped estuary
feeding out at
borderless
crossing broken
into packets, punching

lullabies with
blue beet
lollipop.

Techniques of the Observed

It's a beautiful boat
that doesn't float
or admit its ambling
conjectures. Once I met
a man on a hill, not
once but with a strained
insistence, and I had
never been there, or it
was in a dusky, steaming
underpass and the bridges
were unprotected. There's
not much else to still
the loss or gash or temporary
flurry that doesn't
counterenact. Jelly the
jaybird, salt the sip
as you let down your
slip: a flawed ride's
better than smoothed, lest
you know you're there.

Mall at Night

There is no shade in the forest
when we beat our wings against the moss
& tear the petals off the spruce
revealing what's never said but
spoken, companion to discordant facts
stacked three-foot high above the drawers
clogging corridors. Consonance is this
world's only comfort, stony stare of
stars on bleary night, awake enough
to lose a dozen threads, invent a baker's
dozen more for recompense. The gravel
does not hold, the road beyond repair,
yet closer to, by far, than dusk's approaching
glare.

Under the Pink Tent

Focus
& the light under the shade
begins to focus
back, the
sand underneath,
with a runcible
grin, denotes
what's out past scrambles—
the lost wax of the module
I
had never been,
nor adhered to—
percolations of silhouette
projection, slurred by
ruinous ridges, rumpled
privileges.

"Get Real"

"It doesn't have to be pretty it just
Gotta be a rock." The limbs of the clown
Exfoliate exponentially
Forming a clock. Then the border she lifts
As the fleet comes to town. My gazebo's
Lost, never to be found! Some talk of frowns
Others can't step down; listless, adrift
They mostly mock and pound. Whenever gusts
Return my stare I'm loath to muss the clouds
Encoved without care, queering up the sound.
Charlsey-come-lately, silly just the same
Brittle as booming clangs before a frame.
Give me something hot to eat, a round of
Bread, a heal of meat, then bang & slap
Sluice beats—no delay, synaesthetic'ly.

Palinode

The boy skates in the meadow but all the
same we are hounded by inadvertence.
By the time it tolled, it was half past any
chance of doing anything about it.
Or else the wells get the better of us,
part-advancing beyond entropics, mired
in the distance of increduilty—
plump and green eyesores of immediate
reparation. Sliding down the back of
a telegenic circus pole, eyeing
the background with cartfulls of curio-
sity, ashamed to feel guilty, with no
sense of wrong, just the dizzying delay,
reduplication of expectation.

Social Pork

What a flimsy excuse for denial—
The whole hog attenuates the ceremonial
Blotted artery of common fork
Or wheel and be spun
Over the mountains of dilapidating
Incorrigibilities till the twine
Warps the broken hearts in
Bundles for periods well in excess of
Berserk Baalzebubs, bickering balks—
Deriding only the fuel gage never the
Fire raging inside or crushed
In a regime of ice.

Sunset Sail

Blessed are the narrow who slide
among cracks and build monuments to
slats. For long have I awaited
such news as now passes comment—
news of my comrades lost long
at sea. It was in the following winter
that word was received in a foreign
tongue that one who had refused
solace for some these fifteen months
had taken the hand of his born
foe and danced the Hokey Pokey with
the abandon of clues at
sunset. Such light that fails
me, like sticks in mission
sand, voracious melody of
hardly heard vibrations, potable
allegiance subsumed in the tube.

Swelled by Certainty

There are times
It bumps & then it turns
Around, full carriage against
The wind, bellowing
Stutter, slumber, hoes
In increment by met
Is blossom, heated to
Lecturn, short of
Reversal, gunned in the
Gust—gush—gulp

The Iron Ring and the Ecstasy

I never met a man I liked
Nor woman who liked me
But Love's not grace it's Song
& Life's not long it's Story

The Frontier's not too Far they say
But hardly a boat will go the Way
Once there was a Ferry though
No bridge spans half the Bay

Let's make Amends & say we're friends
I Know that friends don't Lie
Let's take a trip to Alabaster Tip
& say that we have Tried

No boat to sail, no plane to fly
No feet to walk or run
Still where there's Fashion hope remains
Hope that does not Hide

Custom Blinds

I belittle myself by insisting on
a modicum of inversion in every
slash I weigh: fear, as when
dusted by notion of enclosures
jarred by premise, of a wheel
without axle or jimmy with
no foam. Pleated at the corner
of inebriate and swallow, jilt
& tarry, thorns pry loose the
want in taverns of lidded
avenue—gust in the spoons
eye view of wincing procurement
or let down easy, surfacing among
charred charms of scopophilic
ardour.

Revolutionary Poem

Take this

split (splint

of sound

mumbling

murky dormer

as in

Pinky Swear

Such mortal slurp to strain this sprawl went droopy
Gadzooks it seems would bend these slopes in girth
None trailing failed to hear the ship looks loopey
Who's seen it nailed uptight right at its berth
There's been a luring and a ladling lately
That swills the pitch and hiccups fates gone dim
With gumption and such buckle-bursting hurt
Allies with pomp paraded, permed and soapy
You'd guess the call was made by that same twerp
Destroyed the rig and left you almost dopey
    Let daze frequent a thought that's soft and gloopy
    Fluttering like a drill 'een here and earth
    Then spin a phrase or spill a toast in verse
    Such swivel cups the sail of tusked whoopee

Are You Being Sarcastic?

Feathers to caps
like sleep to
snorers, as when
a band mobs
slit, accelerating sash
for potion, deliberate dew
flashing on so-called
slide jam. Rummaging in
storage lockers
of surreptitious hemorrhage,
hampering predilection for
deferral on the decks
of an indiscernible
revelation.

■

The Ache of the Archivist

after Derrida after Freud

In due course, in order to expose
For nothing—an entire interrogation
Vertiginously staging stories. Why
share, cursing jerkily, even if
speculation is never a mute desire?
The very thing forgets its phonolytic
principialities, dribbling illusions beyond
Apparatus, natural rocks, spontaneity of
Witness—the machine, memory, movement.
(These are all inessential affects—

Residual Rubbernecking

Press the key you wish to define
now. Later, outside, you can say
the slosh is softer this year, or
mercy loops its own trail, mucking
through the triumphant pillars of
mastery—moment's solace, forfeiture's
plenitude. I'd wave my hand maybe
four or five times before noticing
that I was asleep, cascading in the blue
mist far from the sash and saddle
of another march down the self-
same street, the paddy without
wagon that hoes its emblematic
embrace. Far, too, from the fissure
in the cracks of what determines our
reconciliation (lubricous
assimilation of convocation). The stick
no longer mangles its allure, if not
justification, which scrambles a little
faster every time you lunge to grab it.
Enough for now, or the now that
yesterday promised, mobbed by angles,
abandoned to insistence.

The Dog Is Dead

A friend of mine named Rudy Loop
Says time's the noblest thing
I think I know better when I say
I prefer soup to stew

The sandpiper knows not where to nest
A bee can find no bone
The baby never stops crying
But I must have my lunch

Hard Copy

To be tutored by the rain & still care for darkness—
not restraint, exactly, where the fall of the window
prefigures an older tale of teeming advertence—
the lock on the meadow or frame around the bee.
Pleading for more, at more steady intervals, not this
plush of void followed fast upon a famine of
probe. The chair retains the moisture
of a time before your own, & then rush
to catch up to its wake; the dew point passes
unsubject to mercy or the course of gain. But
not to lace so bald a pin: to hide in
full view is all that is required of you. Stand
on guard, let others take the fall—she also serves
who wades.

Have Pen, Will Travel

It's not my

business to describe

anything. The only

report is the

discharge of

words called

to account for

their slurs.

A seance of sorts—

or transport into

that nether that

refuses measure.

Rivulets of the Dead Jew

Fill my plate with *boudin noir*
Boudin noir, boudin noir
Fill my plate with a hi-heh-ho
& rumble I will go

Don't dance with me
'til I cut my tie
Cut my tie, cut my tie
Don't fancy me 'til
The rivers run dry
& a heh & a hi & a ho

I've got a date with a
Bumble bee, bumble bee
I've got a date with a
wee bonnie wee
& ahurtling we will go

Edlin

this was what I knew
when all the world grew pale
a little girl had thrown her wing
and I was but a bale
pasted to a patterned frown
or dense with juried mat
for all around I hear it pry
and bear with promise fragrant cant

Charles Bernstein

Charles Bernstein is Director of the Poetics Program at the State University of New York at Buffalo. He is the author of three collections of essays, *Content's Dream* (Sun & Moon Press), *A Poetics* (Harvard University Press), and the recent book *My Way: Speeches and Poems* (The University of Chicago Press). He is the author of over twenty books of poetry, including *Dark City, Rough Trades, The Sophist, Islets/Irritations,* and *Controlling Interests.* Bernstein is also executive editor of The Electronic Poetry Center—epc.buffalo.edu.

*

The Contemporary Arts Educational Project, Inc/Sun & Moon Press is a non-profit corporation dedicated to the publication and presentation of modern and contemporary literature and visual and performing arts. The following individuals have helped, through their contributions, to produce this publication and support other activities of the Project. The Project and its directors are deeply grateful for their generous support.

Steve Allen (Los Angeles, CA)
Jesse Ausubel (New York, NY)
Sherry Bernstein (New York, NY)
Howard N. Fox (Los Angeles, CA)
Marjorie and Joseph Perloff (Pacific Palisades, CA)

The Pomerantz Family (Rosalyn, NY)
Standard Schaefer (South Pasadena, CA)
Milton Stanson (New York, NY)

If you would like to contribute to The Contemporary Arts Educational Project, Inc. please write us at 6026 Wilshire Boulevard, Los Angeles, California 90036 or call us at 323-857-1115.

order from:
Consortium Book Sales & Distribution
1045 Westgate Drive
St. Paul, MN 55114-1065
800-283-3572

Individuals may order direct from:
Sun & Moon Press
6026 Wilshire Boulevard
Los Angeles, California 90036
(323) 857-1115; FAX (323) 857-0143